RAILS, TALES AND TRAILS

A step-by-step guide to **secret locations, fascinating people** and **historic towns** of the old **Central Pacific Railroad** from Sacramento to Reno

by Bill George

Nimbus Films
4520 Shari Way, Granite Bay CA

D1534493

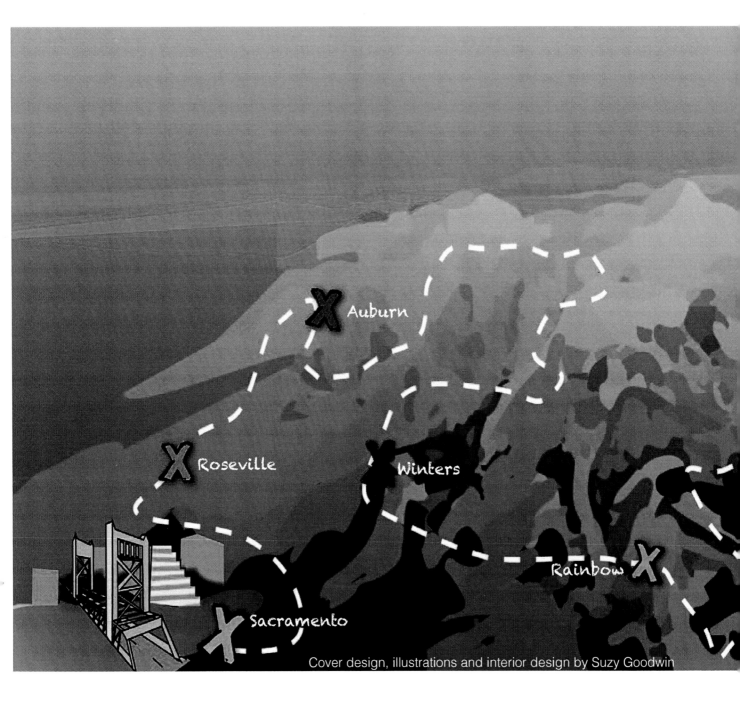

Cover design, illustrations and interior design by Suzy Goodwin

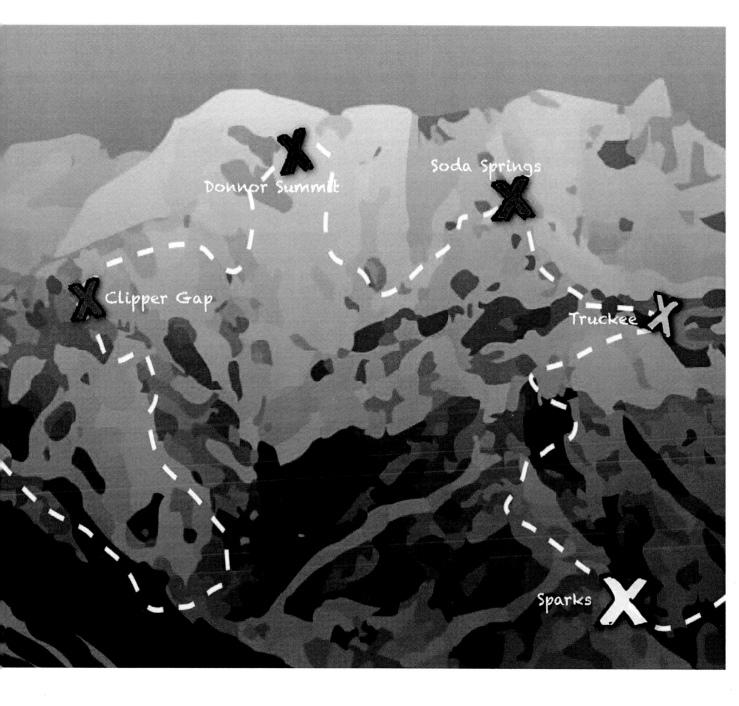

Safety Warning and Disclaimer

I was surprised to learn that a person or vehicle is hit, on average, every three hours by a train. This is a guide to scenic sites that can easily be seen from public areas. Stay off railroad property! Only cross tracks at marked public crossings.

Trains take a LONG time to stop, so keep well clear of them.

For tips on rail safety, please visit Operation Lifesaver, a non-profit organization promoting rail safety.

This book details travel in high, often remote country over rivers, rocks, mountains and hills. Use every precaution and COMMON SENSE. The author has made every effort to ensure accuracy in all details, descriptions, and directions; however there may be factual or typographical mistakes. Conditions can change, roads closed or washed away, and museums and stores and restaurants mentioned here can close. Information is only current up to the date of publishing. Much of the information presented here is based on the author's personal experience, notes and recollection. The purpose of this book is to inform and entertain. The author and publisher shall have no liability or responsibility for any alleged or actual harm or injuries, loss or damage caused, or alleged to be caused, directly or indirectly by the use of information derived from this book.

Dedication:

To my Grandfather,

General Robert E. Moffet, winner of the Distinguished Service Cross, Purple Heart, the Bronze Star,
the American Defense Service Medal, Asiatic-Pacific Campaign Medal,
European-African-Middle Eastern-Campaign Medal, WWI Victory Medal, WW II Victory Medal,
Army of Occupation Medal (with Germany clasp) National Defense Service Medal.

And my Father,
William T. George, Sr.,Navy hospitalman-corpsman attached to E Company, 2nd Marine Battalion,
1st Marine Division and endured some of the most ferocious combat of the Korean War.
He was awarded the Bronze Star for advancing into a minefield to administer medical assistance to wounded marines while under devastating enemy fire.
He was also awarded the Purple Heart for wounds suffered in combat.

And for G.J. "Chris" Graves,
who took countless hours to show me the old route,
research the stories behind it, and helped me get the history right.

ABOUT THE AUTHOR

Bill George is owner of Nimbus Films, located in Granite Bay, California and Executive Producer of the Hidden Wonder of the World, the Transcontinental Railroad from Sacramento to Donner Summit. He is a member of the National Academy of Television Arts and Sciences, and a judge of the Emmy Awards. He spent 14 years in broadcast journalism, working for television stations in Iowa and California. He covered four national political conventions, major college and professional sporting events and the Loma Prieta Earthquake of 1989. He also worked as manager of global marketing and public relations at Ford Motor Company.
This is his first book.

ACKNOWLEDGMENTS
I am deeply indebted to many who helped with my film and book:
I particularly thank Brendan Compton who was the videographer/director on my film, and an invaluable and knowledgeable guide on this book.

Chris Graves, Mead Kibbey, David Haward Bain, Gus Thomson, Kyle Wyatt, Phil Sexton, Jim Wood, Helen Wayland, John Poimiroo, Paul Hammond, Phil Johnson, Sue George, Charla George, Jon Ellis, Jack Duncan, Lawrence Hersh, Melanie Barton, Roger Staab, Steve LaRosa, Traci Rockefeller Cusack, Michael Otten, Addah Owens, Steve Gangstead, Shelley Chappell, Jerry Blackwill, Anthena Humphreys, Gary F. Kurutz, Catherine Taylor, Bob Bell, Kelly Brothers, Cara Randall, Beverly Lewis, David G. Allen, Alan Hardy, Ph.D, William Burg, Tom Jones, Pekka Liemola, Philip Rose, Jim Harville, Doug Ferrier, Norm Hartman, Aaron Hunt, Dave Snyder, Mike Marando, Eric Carleson, Alton Pryor, Michael Sanford, Mark McLaughlin, Daniel Hartwig.

The Sacramento Area is blessed with many fine institutions that were invaluable in the research behind this book, and supported the film and book project:

Placer County Historical Society
Sacramento County Historical Association
California State Railroad Museum
Leland Stanford Junior University
Stanford University Archives
Truckee Donner Railroad Society
Roseville Historical Society
Sparks Museum & Cultural Center
Central Pacific Railroad Photographic History Museum
California State Library
Capital District State Museums and Historic Parks
Placer-Lake Tahoe Film Office

Railroad Hobbies, Inc.
Roseville Public Library Auburn Placer Performing Arts Center
Native Sons of the Golden West
KVIE Public Television
Colfax Heritage Museum
Union Pacific Railroad
Leland Stanford Mansion State Historic Park
Placerville & Sacramento Valley Railroad
Golden Drift Museum
Donner Summit Historical Society
The Chinese Museum of Northern California
Placer County Economic Development Office
Placer-Sierra Railroad Heritage Society
California State Archives
Placer County Museums Division

TABLE OF CONTENTS

Foreword 9

Sacramento Today 13

Terrain, Weather, Topography 15

Sutter's Fort, Home of the Pioneers 17

State Capitol Building 18

Old Sacramento.................................... 19

B.F. Hastings Building 21

California State
Railroad Museum 22

Old Sacramento riverfront 24

Judah Monument................................ 25

The Associates 28

The Big Four: Assembling Wealth 31

Money, men, iron and time payments 33

Historic train depot............................. 36

The heroic art of John MacQuarrie................ 37

Historic Central Pacific Shops 38

Remembering the Chinese............................ 39

Crocker Art Museum................................ 41

At home with the governor,
the Leland Stanford Museum 42

Where the Sierra Nevada "begins" 43

Ok...So Just Call it... the mountains?........... 44

Roseville's gigantic railyard 45

So that's why we have ski resorts! 48

Rocklin roundhouse.................................. 49

Rocklin to Newcastle............................... 50

Auburn Dam overlook................................ 52

Image maker of the Central Pacific 52

Auburn.. 53

A true wonder, Bloomer Cut 54

Bayley House 55

Clipper Gap 56

Colfax 56

Truth and legend of Cape Horn
and the Chinese workers........................ 58

Secret Town 61

Gold Run 63

Dutch Flat 64

Early rollercoaster,
the Towle Brothers Railroad 67

Placer County's Yosemite, Giant Gap 68

The railroad ghost town at Cisco 71

The lost watchman's house
on Signal Peak on Red Mountain 72

The old, slow and beautiful Route 40 73

Big Bend in the Tahoe National Forest............ 74

Pleasures of the old stagecoach route,
Rainbow Lodge...................................... 75

Twain on the train 77

Soda Springs 78

Tunnels at Donner Summit.......................... 80

The Summit to Donner Lake......................... 86

Pioneer Monument at Donner State Park........ 88

Truckee.. 89

Truckee River Canyon from
Truckee to Nevada state line........................ 91

Boca 93

Floriston.. 93

Missing Gold in Verdi, Nevada 94

Reno, Nevada....................................... 94

Sparks, Nevada.................................... 95

End of an era...................................... 96

"Bring me men to match my mountains,
Bring me men to match my plains,
Men with empires in their purpose,
And new eras in their brains."

Sam Walter Foss

FOREWORD

So much of history seems far away and distant to us. Musty books and faded photos are not the best tools for telling the story of the past. So I was lucky to stumble into a historical project that I could hike, touch and feel. This book began as a result of a question I asked myself: what remains of the construction sites of the great Central Pacific Railroad (CPRR) from Sacramento to Donner Summit? Little did I know that obtaining the answer to that question would take several years of blissful research, hiking the original rail route, discovering clues and piecing together the location of the actual construction sites, many of which time, people and the elements had conspired to conceal. As a result I uncovered some of the most beautiful and scenic spots in California, almost all overlooked today.

As I learned about the location of the sites, I heard about myths, legends and mysteries that surround the railroad and the people who built it. I dug into the details of the stories and the people involved and found them every bit as interesting as the story of the construction.

My effort first resulted in a documentary film, *The Hidden Wonder of the World, the Transcontinental Railroad from Sacramento to Donner Summit.* I spent a large chunk of my career in television news, and I used those skills to make the film.

The film received a very encouraging reception in California, aired on the Sacramento PBS affiliate and won the Sacramento Historical Association Award of Excellence. At the suggestion of Tom Granache, the manager of the gift shop at the California State Railroad Museum, I started work on a guide to the spots described in the film. In so doing, I have fleshed out the stories of the people who worked on the railroad. As I learned more I asked more questions. What happened to the people who built the road, the workers and the executives? What are the towns that sprung up along the road like today? As I dug into the story, fascinating figures, long forgotten but whose work lives on today, emerged from the controversial, shadowy past. I have combined the details of how to get to the scenic railroad spots with the colorful tales that fill out the story. To make it easy to find the historic railroad sites, **I have put the directions in bold.**

I think by walking the original grade, peering into the granite tunnels bored through by Chinese workers and visiting the homes and shops of the Central Pacific's founders gave me much more of an understating of this heroic deed than just reading about it. Civil War Historian Shelby Foote hiked battlefields to get a first hand feel for terrain, vegetation and even weather to better understand the decisions and actions made by the men who fought those epic battles. William Faulkner famously said, "The past is never dead. It's not even past," and I certainly learned the truth of that by standing and putting my fingers in the holes Chinese workers chiseled into granite outcroppings and picking up charred rock that had been sent flying dozens of feet by a black powder or nitroglycerin blast.

Every time I speak to groups about the Central Pacific Railroad, I learn more about the enormous impact the railroad had on America, the West and particularly Sacramento and California. Join me on my mountain gambol, and use this guide to plan one of your own.

It's an experience you will never forget.

INTRODUCTION

It was an era of crisis, conflict and opportunity. In 1862, as the realization that the American Civil War would not end quickly, the United States government decided it was time to make sure the nation's east and west coasts were linked by rail.

On July 1, 1862 President Abraham Lincoln, a former railroad lawyer turned politician, signed the Pacific Railway Act which authorized two competing railroads to build the breathtaking project. Sacramento, the capital city of California, became home to the western portion of the effort and began to organize and operate the Central Pacific Railroad. A group of the city's business leaders would successfully complete one of the most immense engineering and construction feats in the history of civilization, the building of the Central Pacific Railroad from Sacramento to Donner Summit. The ground breaking ceremony for the Central Pacific Railroad was held on January 8, 1863, in Sacramento. They pushed through the mountains and laid track through Truckee (then called Coburn's Station) on June 18, 1868. It was five years of incredible labor and perseverance that changed California and the world.

While the Gold Rush's 49ers put Sacramento on the global map the formation of the Central Pacific Railroad ensured it stayed there. Why did this daunting feat start in Sacramento? As a local newspaper pointed out, the citizens, "through accident and circumstance" possessed the crucial "mining, packing, staging, grading and teaming" skills required to build the seemingly impossible road. They also stepped up with money. When the financiers and bankers of San Francisco rejected the plan as a wild fever dream, and refused to invest in it, "The merchants, saloon men, draymen, and everybody in fact, took an interest in the matter, and took from five to ten and fifteen shares of stock simply to encourage it. They said that if anything came of it, it was bound to make business for Sacramento, and they simply took hold of it to show their interest in the matter," said one of the railroad's early planners and backers.

It was a group of Sacramento businessmen branded through history as the "Big Four," but in reality a larger group of men called "The Associates" who raised the money, recruited the engineering and construction talent and found and paid the workers who built the road. For years before it was built, the railroad plan enjoyed broad local support. City leaders looked hungrily at the concept, knowing a transcontinental rail link would enrich the economy and that many merchants would benefit from increased trade, economic growth and a bit of land speculation. Sacramento newspapers cheered the project on and Sacramento residents and citizens of adjacent counties purchased the bonds that helped finance construction. Through the course of these great actions, Sacramento and the Sierra foothill region put its future on the line in a calculated, highly-leveraged gamble.

Sacramento was also home to a Chinese community that established businesses and commercial establishments in the city by the mid 1850s. The community provided food and lodging for workers who came from China via San Francisco, and who found work in the mines and then on the railroad. The railroad simply would not have been built without the hard work, ingenuity and dedication of the Chinese. I hope to honor them by recounting their incredible achievement in this book.

The bet would pay out unevenly for the individuals involved. The railroad left some enriched with fortunes that rivaled any created by American capitalism; it left others bankrupt and despondent, and

Rails, Tales and Trails

like any new technology it was a force of destruction, forever altering wagon roads and ending old jobs as it created new jobs and entire industries. Over time and in historical terms, a very short time, it created a prosperous region that would grow to become one of America's economic showcases. When the Pacific Railroad opened it provided a way to quickly ship the fruits and vegetables from the Sacramento and San Joaquin Valleys to Midwestern and Eastern megalopolises. It only seems inevitable in hindsight that the region's businesses would develop breakthrough innovations like the first refrigerated cars to keep the produce fresh. Orchards, farms, shops, department stores, saloons, bordellos and churches sprung up. A brisk tourist trade developed. Land speculators lured the shrewd and the gullible to the West with promises of economic opportunity that sometimes stretched the limits of credulity. The Central Pacific built a massive industrial complex, the largest west of the Mississippi, to build and repair locomotives and cars. The Roseville rail yard, just twenty miles east of Sacramento, would rise to become the second largest in the nation and employ generations of Sacramentans. Goods for the entire West Coast would stream down this iron road (really a golden road if there ever was one) and be sent north to Seattle or south to Los Angeles. During World War II men and material, including John F. Kennedy's PT boat, chuffed from the eastern manufacturing centers to the west coast ports through the narrow mountain passes. Long after the last drunken 49er passed out in a mud puddle on a rutted street in Nevada City, Auburn or Hangtown (today called Placerville) the economic benefits flowed from the creation of the Central Pacific Railroad. It was a return on investment not even the most optimistic businessman or politician could have foreseen when the road was created.

This is a record of achievement, accomplished by generations of Sacramentans that should make the region's chest fairly burst with pride. But the legacy of the Central Pacific Railroad and the people who funded, built and worked on it has faded from the region's popular awareness. I have lived and been a news reporter here for almost a quarter of a century and I had never heard of many of the once world-famous names of places within an hour's drive or less of my house; Bloomer Cut, Cape Horn, the Secret Town trestle, Giant Gap, the China Wall — all were unfamiliar to me. You won't find these places in textbooks; Sacramento-area schools don't spend much time on the significance and the influence the Central Pacific had on the region. Modern civic leaders mostly ignore it. When the Sacramento International Airport opened a sparkling new billion-dollar terminal, it hung a giant red rabbit (the term is "art element") from the terminal ceiling. There is no exhibit or artwork to tell visitors that they are visiting the area that conceived and constructed one of the greatest transportation projects in history. This grieves me deeply and I think it's a lost opportunity to tell the region's Homeric tale.

But, as a famous poem asserts, "not all the gods are dead." When you walk the hidden trails and abandoned granite tunnels, you will feel the presence of those giants who built the railroad. I hope an August dawn breaks over you, high in the crystalline Sierra, and finds you staring in wonder and disbelief at what men created with their hands from the cruel and unforgiving mountains. May you glimpse that ethereal figure winging across the hills.

A BRIEF EXPLANATION OF RAILROADS AND NAMES

The building of the first transcontinental railroad was designed as a competition between the Union Pacific Railroad (UP) railroad laying track westward from Omaha, Nebraska and the Central Pacific laying track eastward from Sacramento. The railroads were paid AFTER they laid rail, so the impetus was for speed. As we often say when talking about sports competition today, "these two teams really don't like each other" and the UP and CPRR really detested and tried to thwart each other during the construction.

The Central Pacific Rail road of California also called the "Pacific Railroad" is the famed railroad that was founded by the Big Four of Huntington, Crocker, Stanford and Hopkins in Sacramento in 1861. Those are the men that built the rail route over the Sierra Nevada. They and their workers are the ones who drilled and blasted tunnels through granite, and it is their path we follow in this book.

The CPRR essentially ceased to be in 1885 when it was acquired "by lease" by the Southern Pacific Railroad (SP). The Southern Pacific chugged on until 1996, when the UP, the once-detested rival of the Central Pacific Railroad, took over the western portion of the route. The rail line you pass today or ride on from Sacramento over the Sierra Nevada and all the way to Omaha is owned by the Union Pacific Railroad. That's just a little background to help you decipher a sentence such as "this original CPRR grade runs past the SP station in Colfax where the UP trains are sitting." Oh yeah, the passenger trains are today operated by Amtrak. As far as I'm concerned, Sacramento will always be the proud home of the Central Pacific Railroad.

THE OLD GRADE AND TODAY'S RAIL LINE

I don't think the term "continuous improvement" was coined to describe the Central Pacific Railroad but it probably should have been. Almost since the day it was finished the railroad has worked to straighten the line out so that it can ship goods and people faster. The original grade builders circled around hills, built trestles over canyons and culverts, and bored tunnels through granite mountains dictated by the need to keep the grade at a rise of no more than two percent. The original line also had to follow a path that had water and timber very close at hand, and you will drive through forests of fir, sugar pine, cedar and tamarack as you trace the route. The wood was burned and boiled the water that made the steam that powered the trains. The old wood-powered steam engines simply did not have the motive power for anything steeper and it took about a cord of wood to propel a train 26 miles on the flat land and 12 miles through the mountains. In 1909 under the leadership of the legendary E.H. Harriman the line underwent a major realignment, the result of which is that the original grade can be as much as forty miles off of today's line in Utah and Nevada. In California, however, the old grade in many cases is the EXACT same route the Union Pacific uses today. I have indicated in the text where the line today diverges from the original route, but the two are never very far apart. Railroading has always been an investment-heavy industry and in 2012 the Union Pacific was budgeted to spend $3.6 billion for capital expenditures.

SACRAMENTO TODAY

SACRAMENTO TODAY

Elevation 47 feet

Directions: Six hours north of Los Angeles and two hours east and north of San Francisco, bereft of movie stars, spectacular views and beaches you will find unpretentious Sacramento. Sacramento is often just a quick stop for travelers headed up to or out of the ski resorts and beaches that ring high-mountain Lake Tahoe. Sometimes it seems the city's name should be "Sacramento-on-the-way-to-Lake Tahoe."

Sacramento is off California's glamorous beaten path. Tourists flock to Los Angeles for the beaches, Hollywood glamour, fun and sun. San Francisco glitters in the fog, once celebrated as "Baghdad by the Bay" before recent wars erased that exotic comparative. San Diego, Palm Springs, the Redwoods, Yosemite, all conspire to eclipse the state capital of the most populous state in the union.

For travelers, especially those interested in history and geography, that's really a missed opportunity. Sacramento sits smack in the middle of one of the most fascinating historic, geologic and topographic areas of the world. The Pony Express, the great western migration, the Gold Rush, and first transcontinental railroad all were indelibly forged by the Sacramento region and its people.

Easy day trips from the state capital yield a treasure trove of history and scenery for the tourist willing to work just a little bit for his or her reward. And when the day's touring is done, the city and its suburbs offer all the luxuries and epicurean comforts of the most sophisticated urban areas in the world.

Rails, Tales and Trails

THE TERRAIN, WEATHER AND TOPOGRAPHY

Enormous movements of earth and ocean, billowing volcanoes and massive glaciers sculpted the Sacramento region and dictate travel today.

It is a mere 103 freeway miles from the state capitol building in downtown Sacramento to main street in quaint Truckee, California, an easy drive on Interstate 80 of just an hour and 40 minutes in good weather. By comparison, it's about the same distance and time one would take on a car trip from New York City to Philadelphia, or Milwaukee to Chicago. Going such a short distance usually means a drive with the same weather and topography for the entire trip. Going from Sacramento to Truckee means wending your way through dramatically varied terrain and shocking weather shifts. The road rises from Sacramento's 25 feet above sea level to the Sierra crest at Euer Saddle (two miles north of Donner Pass) 7,239 feet high. That's an average elevation gain of 72 feet per mile. Tracing the transcontinental railroad route, you start in the Sacramento Valley, one of the flattest spots on earth. Sacramento features a mild climate, with a rainy season that usually starts in November and ends in April. Hot, dry summer temperatures can often rise into triple digits, while the winters can be wet, chilly and coated by a thick ground fog the locals call a "tule" fog. The gently rolling foothills look placid and tame, but can deal sleet and ice storms starting around the 2,500 foot level. Climbing higher, you are traversing one of the snowiest locations in America, and the interstate is hit with an average of 20 feet of snow per year. But so-called "wet" years are much worse, and in the 2010-2011 snow season a staggering 61-and a-half feet of the white stuff blanketed Donner Summit. When the Central Pacific was struggling through the Sierra Nevada, it endured the winter of 1866-67. During that frigid year 44 storms dumped nearly 45 feet of snow on the Sierra's upper west slope.

Today, it's not unusual for the highway to be closed for hours by howling snowstorms as state snow plows struggle to clear the deluge. The winter can arrive early, with snow not unusual at higher elevations in September, and can last well into spring. The weather moves southeast -to-northwest. Huge storms build off the Pacific, blast San Francisco with wind-driven rain, hurdle the Pacific Coast Mountain Range that separates the coast from the interior, drop into the Sacramento Valley (at sea level and flatter than Iowa or Kansas) and then begin a steady march into the foothills of the Sierra Nevada. The rain can begin to turn to sleet around 3,000 feet in elevation, and turn to progressively heavier snow as it climbs the slopes. World-class ski resorts ring Lake Tahoe, and when the storms stop skiers and boarders bask in warm sun on their runs down the mountains, Lake Tahoe glimmering at their feet.

Much of the land you will be traveling through is owned by the American citizen/taxpayer and administered by the state of California or Uncle Sam. The Desolation Wilderness and Tahoe National Forest sit on much of the land you will be passing through. They are administered by the friendly but firm U.S. Forest Service. You will also hear about the BLM, that's the Bureau of Land Management, which manages, well, land. Then there's the Bureau of Reclamation, which also manages land and some dams. Lots of federal agencies around and of course there are the California State Parks. If you like camping, check the websites of the groups mentioned above for information on availability and location. Or you can find comfortable lodging in the necklace of towns that stretches from Sacramento to Reno, Nevada.

This is the beautiful, sometimes treacherous path you will follow in your pursuit of history. Bring hiking boots, water, blankets, flashlights and food, and in winter tire chains or four-wheel drive vehicles with high clearance. Rock slides, northern Pacific rattle snakes, bears, coyotes, mountain lions and poison oak await you. The Donner Party was the most famous, but certainly not the last, group of travelers to be fooled by the rapidly changing conditions in the Sierra Nevada. Summer and autumn wildfires can close roads and send plumes of choking smoke into the valley. Sierra storms can pop up quickly and hurl lightning at hikers in the high country. The North and Central Forks of the American River, and the tumbling Yuba River bring a swift current of frigid snow melt hurtling down the canyons. Every spring trails that were in good condition the previous year can disappear or be seriously degraded, altered by the ferocious winter. A misstep can cause a plunge down a sheer canyon wall. If this all sounds a bit overblown remember the author is a former news reporter who spent years covering searches for missing hikers, lost kids, drowned swimmers and other assorted tragedies in the region. One year a pair of Japanese rock climbers settled into a rocky crevice to rest on a summer night. A rain storm hit them and froze their bodies into the side of the cliff before dawn. That's how suddenly conditions can change. The forest can be dense and dark. Play it safe and play it smart and pay attention to fire, storm and avalanche warnings.

SUTTER'S FORT, HOME OF THE PIONEERS

Midtown Sacramento between K and L Streets and 26th and 28th Streets.

Sacramento is fortunate to have well-preserved historical assets that you can walk around and get a feel for the city and people who birthed the Central Pacific Railroad.

In 1841 a Swiss immigrant named John Sutter received a land grant in the Sacramento Valley from the Mexican government. He picked a spot where the swift-flowing American River descended from the mountains and joined the Sacramento River, a mighty tidal stream that wound its way through the delta into San Francisco Bay. He used the land to create a flourishing agricultural empire and named it New Helvetia (New Switzerland.) It remained a dusty, distant province until 1848 when a gleaming precious metal disrupted the world.

In 1847 Sutter sent a rescue party to the infamous Donner Party, who were trapped in a winter storm in the nearby Sierra Nevada. The survivors recuperated at Sutter's Fort, and Sutter became famous for his efforts. New Helvetia became the destination for early immigrants to California. I followed that pioneer trail once, traveling west from Iowa during the month of March. After thousands of miles of cold and snow I passed the glittering white summit, with snow piled twenty feet high from the snowplows that cleared I-80. A half hour later I beheld a marvelous sight, the broad emerald valley shining in the distance. It seemed fanciful to me, like walking out of an old black and white movie into Technicolor. How that scene must have thrilled and lifted the spirits of the pioneers who had struggled for months over the rutted trails, finally looking at the land that would sustain them and their half-starved families.

Most of the pioneers fared well, but fate was not sympathetic to Sutter. In less than ten years after founding the town, Sutter's properties were overrun by squatters, some seeking gold, and the fort is all that remains of New Helvetia. It has been restored to its original pioneer look based on an 1847 map and is well worth taking the tour to familiarize yourself with California and Sacramento's pre-railroad history.

STATE CAPITOL BUILDING

Leland Stanford was Governor in 1863 when the magnificent state capitol building was under construction. He said "an edifice should be constructed…satisfactory of the grandeur of the coming time… surrounded by grounds…with a beauty and luxuriousness that no other capitol can boast." That dream came true when the capitol was finished in 1869 and you can tour the Capitol and surrounding grounds which are framed by **L Street to the north, N Street to the south, 10th Street to the west, and 15th Street to the east.**

Sacramento may have fallen into oblivion if it had not won a spirited, multi-city competition to land the Capitol. Despite recent financial woes, the capitol is beautifully maintained. During session, lobbyists, lawmakers, reporters and armies of protestors, civic-minded groups and advocates for just about anything crowd the wide halls. Tours are every hour on the hour and groups of 10 or more can call and book tours prior to their arrival. The docents will show you the old ceremonial offices no longer in use, explain the hidden historic spots, and, if the legislature is in session, get you a seat in the ornate Senate or Assembly chamber. On the walls hang some of the most important California artwork, much of it from 1870-1970. Also on the walls are portraits of the state's governors. The Jerry Brown portrait, more abstract than the others, seems to get the most comment, but that was painted after his first term in office concluded in 1983. No word if he gets another portrait after his current stint is up. The hulking bronze bear outside the Governor's office is a favorite touchstone for school kids who love to rub his nose. Former Governor Arnold Schwarzenegger, the "Austrian Oak," bought the bear for $20,000 and left him behind when he migrated out of office. One thing you won't find in the Capitol is a statue of Ronald Reagan, the only Golden State Governor to move on to the Presidency of the United States, despite the oft-repeated claim that being elected California's chief executive puts you on the presidential contender short list. One of the best spots to relax is Capitol Park, 40 acres of lawn, memorials, trees, gravel and dirt paths sewn with plenty of benches. There are 800 trees and flowering shrubs, with the most notable labeled with a brief description. You will find Redwoods and the Giant Sequoia here, along with California Fan Palms and the rose garden with 140 varieties of colors and fragrances. A pathway leads all around the capitol building for a pleasant stroll. If you like to walk head west down the wide Capitol Mall to Old Sacramento. You will see the city's landmark vertical lift bridge, the gold-colored Tower Bridge that crosses the Sacramento River and lets big ships and tall-masted sail boats slip majestically under its giant arms.

Unfortunately Capitol Mall is lined with government-style buildings that would have made Soviet Union era architects blush with envy. But the view back toward the Capitol is one to cherish.

OLD SACRAMENTO
East side of I-5 at J Street

Thanks to the region's propensity for flooding on near-Biblical scales, tourists can discover what Sacramento looked like in the mid 19th Century. Sacramento remained little noticed until John Marshall found gold in Coloma, fifty hilly miles east of Sacramento. In 1848, gold fever broke out, and the world headed for Sacramento, many by steamer or sail to San Francisco, then up the Sacramento River by schooner to Sacramento. Here many were outfitted with the pots, pans, picks, shovels and clothes needed to survive in the Gold Country. One block away, Chinese merchants were providing the same services for Chinese miners headed for the gold fields. Sacramento's entrepreneurial merchants flourished, and shops and stores rose on the river wharf to greet the gold-thirsty newcomers. The city, perhaps in karmic retribution for soaking the gold seekers, suffered a series of devastating floods. Its location at the meeting of the Sacramento and American rivers was a boon and a curse; good for transportation and commerce, not so good for staying dry (the city holds the ominous designation of having one of the highest flood risks of any city in the nation.)

Rails, Tales and Trails

Chinese laborers who would later help build the transcontinental railroad built earthen levees in the 1850s, but the flood in the winter of 1861-62 was an unwelcome Christmas present that would prove that the walls of dirt could not withstand all that nature could dish out. Starting on Christmas Eve 1861 storms lashed Sacramento for 45 days. The rivers topped the levees and left many dead. Where a city had stood a "Great Lake" appeared, more than 250 miles long and 20 to 60 miles wide. The city was submerged for three months. New Governor Leland Stanford suffered the indignity of having to be rowed a few blocks to the state capitol for his inauguration, and city leaders feared entreaties from a dry San Francisco would pluck the state capitol from the valley to the City by the Bay. Wet and worried, city leaders used thousands of yards of dirt to raise the old city's street levels and keep the townsfolk's heads literally above water. Over the years, the core business district migrated to safer ground east of the river, and the old city fell into decrepitude.

Now restored, that part of town is today called Old Sacramento, a brick and mortar enclave that preserves the early days. There are many seasonal events that celebrate the region's history held in "Old Sac" every year, so check online and see what's up. Old Sac is located

Rails, Tales and Trails

between the Sacramento River and Interstate 5 on the edge of the modern city's downtown. Redevelopment rescued it in the 1960s, and today the traveler can stroll on cobblestone streets and wooden boardwalks and view the old building facades. The original street level is underneath all this, and today you can descend into old layers of the city, taking guided tours of the underground. On today's street level, cars, pedestrians and old-style horse drawn carriages vie for space on the old town's cobblestone streets. Once dried out, Old Sacramento played an important role in three of America's most prominent historical events: the Pony Express, the Gold Rush and the first transcontinental railroad. Take a walk on the old wood-plank wharf that stretches along the Sacramento River. This is part of a waterway that brought the gold miners and their material possessions from San Francisco to the Central Valley, the jumping off spot to the golden treasure trove in the foothills of the Sierra Nevada. The river schooners later brought iron, engines, and people to build the railroad. There were no manufacturing, iron or steel mills in California. Rails, locomotives, passenger and freight cars had to be shipped by sea from the east to San Francisco, where they were loaded onto smaller river schooners for the trip upriver to Sacramento.

Locomotives were shipped in parts, and had to be assembled on the wharf in Sacramento. Finally the trains were put on the track and could join ox-drawn wagons moving material to the rail head.

One of the last vestiges of the river trade between Sacramento and San Francisco is moored here permanently. In 1984 the Delta King riverboat was renovated at a cost of $9 million. Stop in and have a drink in the ornate bar or stay in this floating hotel with modern lodging amenities, two restaurants offering casual or fine dining, two professional theatres, a wine school, and facilities for weddings and meetings. You will get a sense of the robust river life that helped make Sacramento.

B.F. HASTINGS BUILDING

2nd and J streets, Old Sacramento

The B.F. Hastings building houses the Wells Fargo History Museum in Old

Sacramento and holds more history between its walls than most other American buildings. Built in 1853, the large building was constructed by Benjamin F. Hastings to house his thriving bank. Hastings leased the remaining spaces to various companies and people who would make their mark on California. In 1854 Wells Fargo & Co. rented space, rising to golden prosperity while Hastings faded into obscurity. The Hastings building became the first permanent home of the California Supreme Court, which rendered rulings from the building until 1869. Theodore Judah, who surveyed the Central Pacific Railroad route, had an office on the second floor of the building for a short time during 1855. The Pony Express and The Alta and California Telegraph Companies shared space in the building. This was the receiving station where the Pony Express finished its route in the west, carrying mail all the way from St. Joseph Missouri, 1,966 dusty miles away. The riders actually stopped in Folsom, 24 miles east of Sacramento, and the mail was delivered via the Sacramento Valley Railroad the final 24 miles. The teen-age riders averaged 196 miles a day for ten grueling days crossing vast rivers, shining mountains and swollen rivers. A statue of a Pony Express rider, hurtling across the frontier, stands kitty-corner across 2nd and J Streets, memorializing the heroic delivery of the U.S. Mail to this historic corner. The Pony Express lasted just a year and a half, when on October 24, 1861, the first transcontinental telegraph message was received in the **Pioneer Telegraph Building at 1015 Second Street.** The Pony Express ceased to exist two days later, the boy riders forever replaced by iron wires.

CALIFORNIA STATE RAILROAD MUSEUM
111 "I" Street, Old Sacramento

The crown jewel of Old Sacramento is the California State Railroad Museum, one of the most popular museums in America. Visitors come from all over the world to tour it. Inside the spacious and attractive main building, you will find twenty-one beautifully restored locomotives and cars, with helpful and learned docents on hand to explain the exhibits and answer questions. Upon entering, transcontinental railroad fans will enjoy the first exhibit, which features a full-scale diorama of an 1860s-era construction site. The figure standing on the floor doing the survey is Lewis Clement, who surveyed the hardest part of the route through the Sierra. Above him are Chinese workers drilling holes into granite walls high in the Sierra Nevada. This gives visitors a life-like glimpse into the daunting task workers and engineers had in putting the Central Pacific Railroad through the Sierra.

Also inside is the Central Pacific's *Governor Stanford*, also called No.1, the first locomotive to work on the Pacific route. It has been restored to a shiny luster that belies its life as a stolid workhorse. It was manufactured by Richard Norris & Son of Philadelphia, and purchased for $13,688, shipping to Sacramento included. In late 1862 the pieces of the 56,000 pound locomotive were loaded into crates and sent by ship for the four-month trip to San Francisco,

Rails, Tales and Trails

where the components were reloaded onto the river schooner *Artful Dodger* for the trip up the Sacramento River, finally arriving October 5, 1863. The pieces were immediately assembled on K Street, and the locomotive began a long and storied career. Its first mission was handling some of the most important railroad commodities of the day, California politicians. After an excursion featuring a champagne celebration to impress the politicos, No.1 was put to work hauling men and material to the construction site at the railhead and back. It probably traveled no more than 15 miles an hour, but in the era of horse and oxen-drawn wagons, that seemed like light speed. The engine would labor in the Sierra until 1895, when it was con-

demned as "worthless." Unceremoniously retired, it heroically survived a number of close encounters with the scrap heap, residing for years in obscurity at Stanford University and then in a grocery store warehouse. It is almost a miracle that it sits in the railroad museum today, immaculately restored, proudly polished, silent testimony to the glories of the Gilded Age. Look and wonder at this "mighty-mite," which pound for pound may well have been the most productive, and famous, train engine in the world.

Rails, Tales and Trails

Another display you will want to see celebrates the completion of the transcontinental railroad. On May 10, 1869, the Last Spike of the Transcontinental Railroad was ceremonially driven into a polished California laurel railroad crosstie at Promontory, Utah. This symbolic final spike captured America's popular imagination. Until recently, very few people (historians included) were aware of a "lost" golden spike. In early September 2006, this fabled "Lost Spike" went on permanent display at the California State Railroad Museum. Never before in American history had such a simple object won universal recognition as a national icon.

It is exhibited adjacent to Thomas Hill's epic oil-on canvas painting, *The Last Spike*.

The museum also houses a collection of over 60 artifacts excavated from Chinese campsites along the railroad route. Earthenware jugs, glazed ceramic bowls and teapots and a jade ink pallet tell the story of the Chinese workers who supplied much of the workforce that blasted through the mountains

The railroad museum offers many more displays on different themes and eras in American railroading, and you can easily spend a day or more absorbed in the pleasant surroundings. For those who want to dig deeply into the Central Pacific Railroad, a trip to the museum's permanent collection is in order. That facility was being moved in 2012 to a 265,000 square foot facility at McClellan Park (formerly McClellan Air Force Base). The new collections facility will feature a public research space, and it is best to call ahead to reserve some time.

Old Sacramento Riverfront

There is much more transcontinental railroad history to experience in Old Sacramento. Just a few feet outside the museum door you can see and get a feel for what the area looked like when it gave birth to the western portion of the transcontinental railroad. Next to the Sacramento River on a raised wood plank sidewalk are some old wooden buildings. Here you will find the reconstructed Central Pacific freight depot. The first trains worked to move workers and equipment to the railhead, so public amenities for passengers were not much of a consideration. The railroad simply converted an old tool shed into a ticket office while passengers huddled under an overhang for shelter from the elements. Still the railroad was a hit, and in May, 1864 the Central Pacific carried 8,900 passengers as far as modern-day Roseville. Walking around the wooden sidewalks gives you a feel for the earliest days of Sacramento rail freight and passenger service.

Right next door to the Railroad Museum is the **Big Four Building**, named for Collis Huntington, Charles Crocker, Leland Stanford and Mark Hopkins who earned a living in the dry goods and hardware businesses before hatching plans—and making millions of dollars—in railroading. Docents are very friendly and knowledgeable and show how old implements, like hand-cranked drills, helped power the road's construction. The store features other tools and products used during the 1850s and 60s. In the back of the store is a tiny but fascinating exhibit

Rails, Tales and Trails

with information on the manufacturing practices of the 19th century. Pictures of the original Central Pacific Railroad owners gaze at you as you spend time in the comfortable surroundings. The display gives you an understanding of the tools of the time, and the fact that they were powered mostly by people or animals. It is the tools here that built the tracks, staves, trestles and bridges needed to construct the transcontinental railroad.

JUDAH MONUMENT,
2nd and L Streets, Old Sacramento

A few blocks from the museum at 2nd Street and L streets, almost hidden on a tiny patch of lawn, is a marvelous, 20-foot high monument honoring the genius who conceived, plotted, publicized, sold, lived and even died creating the great road, the famed engineer Theodore Judah. Most people don't even notice the monument as they ride past. But it is worth some time on your visit to examine the monument's symbolic detail. You will notice pine trees pointing to a bridge spanning a wide crevasse. A tunnel cuts through the granite of the Sierra Nevada as the road wends its way higher and higher through seemingly impassable alpine terrain. One is moved by the fact that this monument was paid for by the workers of the Southern Pacific Railroad during the Great Depression, thanking Judah for creating the business which supported them and their families for generations.

The plaque reads:

> *"That the West may remember Theodore Dehone Judah, pioneer, civil engineer and tireless advocate of a great transcontinental railroad America's first. This monument was erected by the men and women of the Southern Pacific Company, who, in 1930, were carrying on the work he began in 1860. He convinced four Sacramento merchants that his plan was practicable and enlisted their help. Ground was broken for the railroad January 2, 1863, at the foot of K Street, nearby. Judah died November 2, 1863. The road was built past the site of this monument, over the lofty Sierra - along the line of Judah's survey - to a junction with the Union Pacific at Promontory, Utah, where on May 10, 1869, the last spike was driven."*

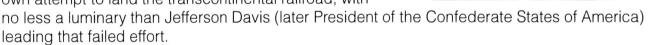

The statue was sculpted by John MacQuarrie, an artist and sculptor of heroic, monumental art who we will encounter a few more times on the route.

How did Judah pick the route? The ancient Greeks said you could find a path through mountains by loading a hundred pounds on a burro and following as it picked a path. Judah, a trained and experienced railroad surveyor, was much more methodical and had the benefit of many previous surveying parties who had explored possible transcontinental routes. With slavery the burning issue of the day, Union supporters were determined to find a route through the North. The South waged its own attempt to land the transcontinental railroad, with no less a luminary than Jefferson Davis (later President of the Confederate States of America) leading that failed effort.

Theodore Judah was that rare bird, a visionary engineer who could lobby politicians, buttonhole business tycoons for sales pitches, and promote his project to the public. In a publicity stunt that would be the envy of any large public relations firm today, he took a room in the U.S. Capitol and turned it into a Pacific Railroad "museum" to "educate" members of Congress about his scheme.

It was in Old Sacramento that Judah sold the idea of the transcontinental railroad to local investors, but only after he had been shut down by the big money boys in San Francisco, who refused to bite on his $70,000 stock offering. Called "Crazy Judah" by the San Francisco sophisticates, Judah returned to Sacramento and met the team that would form the core of the project, Leland Stanford, Collis P. Huntington, Mark Hopkins, and Charles Crocker. Crocker's brother, Edwin "E.B." Crocker was also an important early player and would provide legal advice to the Big Four. Also present at the creation were Dr. Daniel Strong, Lucius A. Booth, jeweler James Bailey, Cornelius Cole, later congressman and senator from California, and B. F. Leete, one of Judah's surveyors. On the 28th of June 1861 the "Central Pacific Rail Road" of California was incorporated, however cautiously. The new investors would only pay for the remaining mountain surveys, then evaluate the situation. Judah convinced them that if the railroad failed, at least they would have a wagon road over the mountains to tap into the lucrative Nevada mining trade. The San Francisco investors would not go gently into the night, and in fact spent the next several years hollering about the deal that never was. Having passed up a chance to make hundreds of millions, they began publicly and privately sniping at the

Rails, Tales and Trails

Sacramento rubes, promoting alternative routes and charging the Big Four with crime, corruption and all sorts of wicked perfidy. Who in San Francisco rejected Judah? Could it have been the Wells Fargo Company? Judah had told his wife that when he was in San Francisco, "I have one of the richest concerns in San Francisco into it." We all know the famous Wells Fargo symbol: the stagecoach. Wells had a stronghold on the express shipping business in the West before the transcontinental railroad was incorporated. Wells also had a strong banking presence, so it was one of the richest corporations in California. Judah was a smart, tenacious promoter. He would logically have gone to see Wells Fargo while in San Francisco, or in Sacramento where Judah and Wells Fargo at one time shared the same office space. In hindsight it may have been a missed opportunity for Wells Fargo, although the banker and the railroad both remain in business.

It was in Sacramento that geography provided a break in typical Sierra topography that the builders could take advantage of. The rivers descended from the mountains, flowing uniformly east to west. They cut canyons with firm ridgelines that rise gently uphill, shadowing the American River. As you drive along Interstate 80 you will see the ridges running for miles with scarcely a gap. The Sierra here has been described as a series of curling waves, similar to ocean waves that surfers love to ride. It was precisely the slope needed to ascend the Sierra. Or so Judah believed. Judah did not finally settle on the Donner Summit route until his survey of the Sierra in 1860-61, when Doc Strong, a Dutch Flat druggist, showed him how the ridge line between the Yuba River and the North Fork of the American River would provide a suitable grade from Dutch Flat over Donner Summit. This "Truckee route" had actually fallen into disuse well before the end of the Gold Rush. The Truckee route was difficult for wagon trains to climb up from the east, so the wagon trains of the mid-1800s sought lower mountain passes that were easier for wagons and walking pioneers. But Judah was surveying for a railroad, not a wagon train. He saw that a large labor force could build the trestles and tunnels needed to make it up the western slope of the Sierra. This momentous decision allowed Donner Pass to regain the transportation supremacy that it holds to this day, as you will discover when you travel up the slope.

Modern surveys done with the assistance of satellites confirm he picked the best route. In 1863 Judah died of fever on a trip back east before construction had begun in earnest. He was 37 years old.

THE ASSOCIATES

Old Sacramento is where the Big Four of Stanford, Huntington, Crocker, Hopkins came together to change history. The names sing of prestige and rank, of American aristocracy. To this day some of America's most prestigious and influential institutions reflect their names: Stanford University, the Crocker Art Museum and San Francisco's classy and elegant Mark Hopkins Hotel, perched atop The City's prestigious Nob Hill.

They left some of the biggest footprints on California, its history and terrain, but none of them were born in the Golden State. They would, collectively, become politicians, lawyers, shop-keepers, philanthropists, builders, stock salesmen, borrowers, lenders, shippers, land sales-men, wagon road owners, negotiators, and, some charged, bribers, political wire-pullers, cheaters and frauds. They had barely started running trains on the tracks from Sacramento when they filled excursion trains full of newspapermen, politicians, wine and bourbon, and took them on jaunts through the hills in order to curry favor with opinion makers and the elite. When they got wind the Speaker of the House of Representatives was on the way west to inspect their construction, they renamed the town at the railhead (Colfax) in his honor. The inspection went amazingly well. For a long time they were probably the most hated people in San Francisco and had an entire newspaper devoted to chronicling their every move in a critical light. Ambrose Bierce (a lesser known but much more venomous writer than his con-temporary Mark Twain) hurled verbal thunderbolts at them.

Rails, Tales and Trails

There would be investigations, inquiries, Congressional hearings, reports by muckraking journalists, and even novels dedicated to exposing them for their supposed perfidy. It was an era of political corruption and payoffs that would be known, thanks to Twain, as "The Gilded Age." But when the investigations ended and the ink for the purple prose ran out, the Big Four remained standing, not one of them indicted for anything. The cynics said they were just good at covering their fraud-sodden tracks.

They helped create and develop California's tourism and agriculture industries. Most of their employees, including the Chinese, seemed to like them, or at least tolerate them, but what worker "loves his boss?" At a critical time in California's economic development they provided jobs, paid big wages in gold coin, and employed tens of thousands of people. The Big Four all rose from modest means, created great wealth, and built fabulous mansions, three of which were destroyed by the 1906 San Francisco earthquake. They met payroll every month and were known for paying bills on time. During construction they were in constant motion: construction Boss Charles Crocker living with his family at the head of the grade, making sure the heavy lifting was done, and done right; Leland Stanford, who was elected California Governor, courted the politicians including a certain friend of the Railroad named Abraham Lincoln, and later hurried out to Salt Lake City to parley with Brigham Young; Collis P. Huntington, the financer, playing every card in the deck to get loans and bonds, scheming to outwit his enemies at the Union Pacific and other railroads, beating them in the race to buy rails, engines and cars before his competitors could. Hopkins was quieter, less dynamic, and older than the others but the one they ultimately looked to for final approval on projects. In business together for some forty years, they alternately damned and praised each other in the normal practice of seeking glory for things gone right and deflecting blame when disaster struck. Seeking history's approval they left reams of letters, stacks of reports, scores of statements and journals. This literary record created another booming industry for historical researchers, reporters, authors, publishers and booksellers that remains a vibrant source of employment for people bad at math to this day.

Rails, Tales and Trails

The Big Four referred to themselves as "The Associates," a name so bland one wonders if it was purposely employed to mask their dynamic nature. History, which often gets labels wrong, made a necessary correction, to which I have added a powerful adjective; they were not The Associates, they were the Big Freaking Four. But in the beginning they were just shop keepers in a muddy town on the fringe of the Gold Rush.

THE BIG FOUR, ASSEMBLING WEALTH

Collis P. Huntington

He was born with little in the way of material wealth, but Collis P. Huntington had displayed early entrepreneurial talent as a 49er on his way to the gold fields, his intent to be a merchant not a miner. Taking all he had including his grubstake of $1,500, he took the crowded route from New York over the Isthmus of Panama to the Pacific, then north to San Francisco. When ships failed to materialize on the Pacific side of the voyage, thousands of people were stuck on the rainy, muddy, mosquito-and disease-infested crossing. In order to get supplies to the needy travelers, 22-year-old Huntington, six-feet tall and muscular, hiked the isthmus 24 times to get goods from the Atlantic coast to the 49ers stuck at a town on the Pacific side of the crossing, a distance of about 50 miles on a winding, hilly, nasty route hacked out of the jungle. The work paid off and when he was able to leave Panama he had increased his holdings to $5,000. When he finally landed in San Francisco August 31, 1849 Huntington noticed the flotilla of silent ships in the harbor; their excited crews had all abandoned ship and lit out for the gold fields. Avoiding high prices and the high cost of doing business in San Francisco (a refrain that can be heard today) he headed upriver to Sacramento, the gateway to the foothill gold mines. Once again he played the role of supplier, finding goods and getting them to those who needed them. Wearing a large floppy "Panama" hat, dressed for the baking heat, the strapping young man must have been an imposing sight on his travels between San Francisco and the mining camps above Sacramento. He was prospering nicely when fire, a common frontier nemesis, struck Sacramento. It destroyed most of the city, the newly-created "Chinadom" along with the white-owned stores. It was then that Huntington made a friend for life, fellow merchant **Mark Hopkins.** Hopkins, also a New Yorker and a 49er, was eight years older than Huntington, had studied law and run businesses in New York and the foothill community of Hangtown (today called Placerville), 45 miles up the slope from Sacramento, whose very name implied the execution of swift and final justice for those accused of crime. Hopkins

had also been wiped out in the fire, so he turned to his neighbor Huntington and they began a business that would last a lifetime. Clearing the fire debris and absorbing the financial loss, Huntington and Hopkins opened a wholesale grocery at **54 K Street**. Hopkins is the only one buried in Sacramento. You can visit his impressive memorial in the **City Cemetery at 1000 Broadway. Amasa Leland Stanford** arrived in California in 1852, where he joined his brothers working in a general store at Michigan Flat in Placer County. In the rough gold country he earned a reputation as a fair man, settling many a miner's tiff serving as justice of the peace. Stanford moved to Sacramento where he launched spectacular careers in business and politics. An ardent supporter of Lincoln and a staunch abolitionist, He lost an 1859 race for California governor on an anti-slavery ticket. He attended Lincoln's inauguration and prowled the corridors of power in Washington making the case for the Pacific railroad. He became a pillar of the Republican Party in California and was elected Governor in 1862. "Stanford made major constitutional changes, sponsored legislative reforms, backed the conservation of forests, and cut the state debt in half" and worked tirelessly to keep California in the Union. He also found time to help found and organize the fledgling Central Pacific Railroad, serving as president. His accomplishments are almost too numerous to mention, but here are a few: President of the Western Pacific Railroad, President of the C&O Railroad, President of the Pacific Mutual Life Insurance Company, President of the Occidental and Orient Steam Ship lines, President of the Bodie Bluff Construction Mining Co. He ran mines, oil companies and helped organize Sacramento's library. He owned two wineries, and a vineyard that at the time was the largest in the world, bred horses and was a life member of The California Academy of Sciences. In 1885 alone he was elected to the U.S. Senate, founded Stanford University, by land mass the largest University in the world with the biggest private endowment (approximately $1 billion) ever, and became President of the Southern Pacific Railroad.**Charles Crocker** was another native New Yorker. Crocker got to California on the overland route, bumping across the plains and straining up and over two mountain ranges to reach California at age 28. He would later turn that route from wagon rut to iron and steel railroad. He also tried his hand at mining, and then turned merchant. Crocker became construction boss of the road, actually living at the rail head with his wife to personally supervise construction. Big, burly, enthusiastic, he met every challenge, and brought the road in seven YEARS ahead of schedule, despite the fact he had never built a railroad before. "I had all the experience necessary. I knew how to manage men; I had worked them in the ore beds, in the coal pits, and worked them all sorts of ways, and had worked myself right along with them," he explained. In 1865 he would hire Chinese workers to push the project through the mountains.

MONEY, MEN, IRON AND TIME PAYMENTS

One of the biggest and continuing controversies about the transcontinental railroad is the government's involvement in financing the project. For more than 150 years critics, both liberal and conservative, have argued that federal "subsidies" and giveaways to the railroad were not needed or were overly generous. In 1861 the Big Four, without any government funding, incorporated the Central Pacific Railroad. They authorized and paid for Judah's final surveys. Judah's surveys revealed that fifteen tunnels would be needed, and the average cost of building the line would be $88,425 per mile. There was little manufacturing capability in California. The cost of transporting all the supplies was almost incalculable; all the engines, rail cars, and iron rails were made in the east, and the Panama Canal shortcut did not exist. Goods were shipped all the way around the cape of South America to San Francisco, a jaunt of 16,000 miles. There the cargo was unloaded and packed back onto river steamers that took the material upriver to Sacramento where it was offloaded to platform cars to go into the mountains. Delays, mishaps at sea, and a thousand other factors could conspire to mess up the timing of the deliveries, causing logistical nightmares for the construction crews. Sitting idle cost money, and money was scarce. The Big Four would provide the seed money, but they had nowhere near the capital to build such a monumental railroad. It would cost $23 million to lay 690 miles of track, 130 miles of it through the Sierra Nevada. Where could the Sacramento shopkeepers find that kind of money?

Rails, Tales and Trails

Almost as soon as the railroad was incorporated Judah returned to Washington to lobby Congress for assistance, just as the Civil War was escalating rapidly into a titanic struggle. Congress, as always, found danger lurking everywhere, and one worried legislator fretted that the two railroads would complete just the first parts of the road, leaving a gap in the middle. The congressman came up with the ingenious solution of making the railroads build the first forty-mile stretch in the middle of the country, an impossible task. Reason prevailed and the Pacific Railroad Bill was signed by President Lincoln July 1, 1862. Now the work could be started.

The government came up with money and a whole bunch of strings. Some saw those strings as ropes that the Big Four would use to hang themselves. Construction was financed by thirty-year, six-percent U.S. Government Bonds. They were issued at the rate of $16,000 per mile of tracked grade completed west of the base of the Sierra Nevada (in Sacramento) and $48,000 for tracked grade completed over and within the Sierra Nevada and the Rocky Mountains. As a further incentive, the government followed a precedent that had already been established of granting land to the railroads. The railroad would receive ten square miles of public land for every mile laid, on alternating sides of the line, (it is called a "checkerboard" pattern) except where railroads ran through cities and crossed rivers (then and now the most valuable land.) The idea was to make this wild and worthless land valuable to the government and the rail-road. Critics have howled through the decades that this was an unnecessary giveaway that ultimately cost the federal government billions of dollars. But others point out that the land

Rails, Tales and Trails

was, at the time, largely worthless, winding through wilderness, deserts and mountains that were virtually devoid of people. If you drive from Omaha to Sacramento on I-80 you will still travel past hundreds of miles of empty land. When the railroad was built, it provided the crucial connection that gave value to the government land. The railroad worked (and still works today) to place businesses on that land to use rail transportation, not only boosting the value of the federal government's parcels, but helping create tax-paying businesses and jobs (to this day, you can still get free land from government in America if you can create a business on it.) The initial financial problem was that the Central Pacific was required to build forty miles of road (all the way to Colfax) before it would receive any of the bond money. The investors somehow secured money to get thirty miles of track laid, but then the whole scheme seemed to be coming apart at the seams. The government would not let the railroad sell any bonds on its own. Banks would not lend them money. The Big Four had wagered everything they had and must have longed for the profitable and relatively risk-free merchant existence they previously enjoyed. As Charles Crocker later remembered, "I would have been glad when we had 30 miles of road built, to have got a clean shirt and absolution from my debts. I owed everybody that would trust me, and would have been glad to have them forgive my debts and taken everything I had, even the furniture of my family, and to have gone into the world and started anew." Every shipping delay, every construction screw up, every misplaced shipment of spikes or rail occurred in the face of a giant ticking clock; both the Union Pacific and Central Pacific faced forfeiture to the federal government of all the track, rolling stock, buildings and land if the railroad was not complete between the Missouri River and Sacramento Rivers by Jan. 1, 1874. Critics and enemies must have dreamt of buying the remnants of the failed enterprise for ten cents on the dollar.

The Bill was amended in 1864 to provide a way to fund the building of the road. The railroad was allowed to sell its own bonds, and the land grants doubled to twenty miles. This bill proved the formula for success, and the construction deadline was met, comfortably, in May 1869. The bonds were paid off in 1898 and 1899, when the government collected $63,023,512 in principal and $104,722,978 in interest. That's a return on the initial investment of $64,623,512, and not counting the enormous discount (one source says it was worth $1 billion) the railroads gave the federal government for mail delivery and shipping. "The government," says Kyle K. Wyatt, Curator of History & Technology at the California State Railroad Museum, "received/saved much more money in the deal than the railroads received."

We are ready now to follow the rail route out of the old city. Give yourself plenty of time, at least a day, to explore Old Sacramento, The Railroad Museum and the train depot. Old Sacramento has many fine restaurants and attractions, so it's fun to make a day of it. You may even run into one of the Big Four or their friends strolling the streets who will be glad to take some time and explain in great detail how the railroad was started.

Rails, Tales and Trails

HISTORIC TRAIN DEPOT
401 I Street, Sacramento

Just a few short blocks east of Old Sacramento at 401 I Street is the Amtrak station. Sacramento's Amtrak train station is located immediately adjacent to Old Sacramento and the California State Railroad Museum. Actual walking distance between the Sacramento train station and Old Sacramento is about two city blocks.

The easiest way to get to the station from Old Sacramento is to walk behind the Railroad museum to the paved pathway under the freeway. This is along the same route the original rail route followed.

The station was built by the Southern Pacific Railroad in 1926. It is listed in the National Register of Historic Places. Walk through it today and see the elegant touches that remain from the days when travel by rail was the elegant and refined way to tour the country. Here is an account of the station in its heyday, by *Railroad Age* magazine.

"The passenger station proper is of the Italian type of architecture. It is 370 ft. long, with a width of 54 ft. at the west-end and 128 ft. at the east-end. The Central portion of the building, which houses the waiting room and concourse, is 83 ft. wide. The exterior walls are faced with brick with a mingled light russet color, while a darker russet tiling is used on the sloping roof. The entire building is trimmed with architectural terra cotta and the lines of the structure, enhanced by eight circular topped windows, 35 ft. high and glazed with amber colored cathedral glass, combine with the color treatment of the walls and roof to furnish a harmonious and pleasing aspect." But it is what is inside that captures the most attention. There, above the heads of busy travelers, is a huge, colorful revelation, a mural depicting the groundbreaking for the transcontinental railroad. The scene is a depiction of the January 8, 1863 event, painted 68 years later by San Francisco artist John MacQuarrie, the same artist who sculpted the Theodore Judah statue. It was dedicated August 23, 1931. The *Sacramento Bee* reported, "It is expected that a mate to the painting will be added in the near future," and explained that a bronze plaque describing the scene would be placed under the painting. No such plaque is in the station today, and there is no record of a companion mural. No one knows if those objects were produced, and if so what happened to them.

Who is in pictured on the mural (see page 38)? Some of the most important people in railroad and Sacramento history. The man at the podium speaking with his arm out is Charles Crocker. His hand is over bald-headed Collis P. Huntington. Next to Huntington is Mark Hopkins. Oddly placed to the right of the stage (as you are looking at it) and glowering with his hands behind his back is big, dark-haired Governor Leland Stanford. He is pictured here at a younger age than the other Big Four members, probably when he was governor of California in 1862. Did the artist feel Stanford was a loner, and outsider who did not deserve to be placed on the podium? In front of the stage is a surveyor whom logic suggests is Theodore Judah. The other people in the mural have not been identified by the author.

THE HEROIC ART OF JOHN MACQUARRIE

His legacy was lost over the years, but it would not be a stretch to say that MacQuarrie's work has probably been seen in person by more people than the work of almost any other California artist. His murals hung in train stations during the heyday of passenger train travel.

Born in 1871, MacQuarrie painted murals in train stations between 1909 and 1941. His murals were installed in Salt Lake City, Sacramento, San Jose, Palo Alto, Salinas, Houston and Mesa, Arizona. All survived until recently except the murals in Houston and Mesa, the former lost, the latter destroyed when the depot was torn down. MacQuarrie's murals reflect Western history themes in grand fashion. In 1909 he created two murals that dominate the Union Pacific depot in Salt Lake City to this day. They are *Driving of the Golden Spike* which is a rendering of the famous meeting of the Central Pacific and the Union Pacific at Promontory Summit, and a mural depicting the arrival of the Mormon pioneers in Utah. In 1941 he painted a mural for the Palo Alto Southern Pacific Station. "Its central theme is Leland Stanford's dream of a University influenced by a pageant of transportation. The mural depicts facts and events of significance and influence historically expressed in the development of California," according to the National Park Service's account. Also in 1941, he created the mural in the Salinas depot which includes renderings of World War II era American soldiers, dancing Native Americans in headdress, cowboys and agricultural scenes all set against a speeding train. It is big, bold, colorful and optimistic art, the embodiment of what Americans used to call "progress." Farm fields teem with produce and cattle as wagon trains and cowboys stream past in a pageant of action that would make Arnold Schwarzenegger gasp in astonishment. We will find MacQuarrie later on in the story, literally at the top of the mountain.

HISTORIC CENTRAL PACIFIC SHOPS

Behind the Amtrak station, toward the river, you will see seven immense brick buildings, the remnants of an era when this site was a railcar production and maintenance facility that was the largest industrial center west of the Mississippi. Now, eight Central Shops — seven brick and one metal — are all that remain of what was once at least 243 buildings. Sacramento deeded the railroad thirty acres of slough along the city's riverfront, as well as an adjacent marshy lake variously known as the Old Slough, China Slough, or Lake Sutter. By 1869, the CPRR had filled in twenty acres of the Old Slough and begun construction. Inside the former boiler shop the 68-foot-tall single-story structure is more reminiscent of an ancient cathedral than a modern factory due to the shadowy light that streams into the dark buildings from rows of windows high up the sides of the structures.

These are the first industrial buildings in California, dating to 1867. For decades, workers assembled and repaired locomotive engines in the buildings. At one time, 100 "workshops" as the old industrial buildings were known, stood on this spot. The Historic American Engineering Record's report, conducted by the National Park Service, found that "The shops' original function, steam locomotive heavy repair, ranged from scheduled maintenance such as boiler cleaning and flue replacement, wheel changes, and the like, to repairs of serious damage incurred in wrecks and derailments. But the Sacramento Shops, while dominated by heavy repair operations, were in actuality an amalgam of retrofitting, manufacturing, and maintenance facilities. The shops never focused simply on repair, nor solely on manufacture, at any point in time. Master mechanics, superintendents, foremen, and workers introduced various innovations into equipment, or added new technological advances, such as air brakes, as they became available. They produced a variety of parts for the company's steamships, and for the central storehouse that supplied the entire system as well. They occasionally manufactured items for other companies too, even building a pump for the Sacramento Water Works."

At the peak of activity during World War II, more than seven-thousand people worked there. After World War II work at the yards declined steadily. In 1999, the Union Pacific Railroad closed its last remaining industrial operations at the yards, and demolished many buildings in anticipation of selling portions of the site to developers. Plans to develop the area into a sports and entertainment arena fell through, but the city has vowed that the old shops will be preserved no matter what is erected. The master plan is to create a railroad technology museum that celebrates the history of the railroad as well as railroad technology and science. It may be possible to secure a tour of the site by contacting the railroad museum, but if construction proceeds as planned be prepared to see some dust flying as the area is transformed.

REMEMBERING THE CHINESE

Sacramento Federal Courthouse, 501 " I " Street

You can't miss the massive, modern monolith that is the Sacramento Federal Courthouse, just across 5th Street from the old rail yards. From its top floors you can get an excellent view of the old industrial buildings in the rail yards. In 1994 researchers from Sonoma State University carried out archeological testing on the block the courthouse was to be built, the spot of the last surviving portion of Sacramento's mid-19th century Chinese district. The project unearthed pottery, fish and animal bones and other implements of daily life that shed light on how the Chinese lived day-to-day and what their relationships with the Anglo community may have been like. There is a small display in the lobby of the courthouse with a few shards of Chinese pottery and bowls. Keep in mind you will have to go through a metal detector to get to the display. Here you will learn about "China Slough." Chinese lived around

the lake for a half century, starting in 1850. It bordered on the north-east portion of Old Sacramento. One fact that usually surprises people when I talk about the Chinese experience working on the transcontinental railroad is that thousands of Chinese were living and working in California for 15 years by the time the Central Pacific Railroad hired them in 1865. By 1852, 25,000 Chinese had reached "Gold Mountain," their name for California. The Chinese called Sacramento Yee Fow, or Second City, and San Francisco Dai Fow, Big City. In order to pay for passage to California, Chinese workers indentured themselves to Chinese brokers who had control over them until their debts were paid. These merchants formed the "Chinese Six" companies in California, including the Yeung-wo, Sam Yap, and Sze Yap, which were located in San Francisco with branches in Sacramento. The companies formed "Chinese Consolidated Benevolent District Associations," and built boarding houses that controlled almost every aspect of Chinese life in California. One contemporary account of a boarding house says the "upper story and the attic were filled with lodgers, nearly all of whom were staying temporarily on a visit from the mines or on their way to or from China." The Sze Yap reportedly contained a hospital in Sacramento, and other houses provided "beds, fuel and water to guests who remain but a short period; also a lodging place and medicines for the infirm, aged and sick." The houses had strict rules; no gunpowder, stolen goods, no filth or bathing, no trash, rags, fighting or noise, no baggage allowed for more than three years, and one luggage chest to a person. The association staff would do the hard work of preparing and serving food. Meals were served on tableware from China, and locally produced and sourced meat and vegetables were supplemented with sauces, oils and fish from China.

While the Chinese formed a community that could obtain its own food and clothing, they also had to establish relationships with American businessmen to secure other goods, and hired them as agents. The business agents fulfilled another function; they could help the Chinese circumvent the heinous discriminatory laws. In 1855 the California legislature made it illegal for Chinese to testify in court, making them easy targets for swindlers who would attempt to take their property in legal "disputes." Seeking legal protection, the Chinese hired agents like Sacramento Alderman Josiah Gallup to act as a middleman in buying property and homes.

Rails, Tales and Trails

Gallup purchased, then sold, a home and a lot to "Aching & Tongkee" and had the transaction witnessed by six local businessmen. No one would try and use the courts to take the property away from these new owners.

The Chinese worked to influence their Anglo neighbors. In the 1850s and 1860s, as the Big Four were rising to political and commercial prominence in Sacramento, Chinese merchants hosted lavish banquets for Sacramento's movers and shakers, including one meal December 7, 1861, described as a 26-course Chinese dinner with champagne. An admiring newspaper reporter called the affair "first rate." We will pick up the path of the Chinese again in the mountains.

CROCKER ART MUSEUM
3rd and O Streets

Just a few blocks from Old Sacramento is the Crocker Art Museum, one of the most lasting and significant gifts from the founders of the railroad. This was the home of the family of Edwin Bryan "E.B." Crocker, the less-famous brother of the Big Four's Charles Crocker. E.B did quite well and was one of America's richest men when he died. A fervent abolitionist before he moved to California, he had defended runaway slaves. As tensions rose that would lead to Civil War, he joined Leland Stanford to help form California's Republican Party and keep the state loyal to the Union.

A successful attorney, E.B was the general counsel for the railroad. In 1868, he purchased the property and buildings on the corner of 3rd and O Streets. He hired a local architect to design and renovate the home into a grand, Italian villa-style mansion, and added a library and gallery space on the second floor, finishing it in 1872. Today you can walk the floors of the original historic gallery and see the twin curved stairways, imported tile floor and rich polished wood that the era's expert craftsmen installed.

In June 1869, E. B. Crocker suffered a stroke and was forced from his exhausting role as day-to-day operations chief of the CPRR. Still, he was healthy enough to tour Europe between 1869 and 1871, and he and his wife Margaret used his fortune assembling railroads to acquire a massive art collection. A modern critic noted that "though their art did not always reflect careful selection, they amassed a collection of fine European paintings from the 16th to 19th centuries." Art critics seem often to be somewhat snobby. The Crockers returned to Sacramento in 1872 with 700 paintings and more than 1,000 drawings, the largest and finest private American collection of the time. E.B. died in 1875, but Margaret became one of the city's leading socialites. The art gallery, one of the town's most beautiful buildings, became a Sacramento social salon where she hosted parties, events and fundraisers. Celebrity guests of the era like former President Ulysses S. Grant and playwright Oscar Wilde made sure to visit when they came west. In 1884 Margaret donated the gallery and the Crocker art collec-

Rails, Tales and Trails

tion to the city and the California Museum Association, the first public art museum founded in the Western United States. It remains one of the leading art museums in California. Here you will find Charles Nahl's *Sunday Morning in the Mines*, the epic painting of good and evil in the gold fields, dominating the stairwell. Also in a quiet wood-panelled room to the side of a main gallery are portraits of the Big Four by Stephen William Shaw. A 49er, Shaw met Collis P. Huntington when they sailed on the same ship from Panama to San Francisco. You will also find three stunning 1870s-80s brooches (two by Tiffany and Company), a portrait of Margaret Crocker wearing one of the brooches, a hair wreath, and many Crocker family portraits. In 1885 20,000 people jammed the mansion and grounds to honor Margaret's devotion to the arts, charity and Sacramento.

AT HOME WITH THE GOVERNOR, THE LELAND STANFORD MANSION

8th and N Streets

Just a few blocks away sits, or struts, Leland Stanford's Victorian mansion. It's now a state historic park. **Enter through the visitor's gate on N Street located halfway between 8th and 9th Streets.** Follow the brick path to the Visitor Center at the rear of the property. I highly recommend taking a tour, which is offered on the hour without reservations.

This elegant brick home was built during 1856-1857 by prominent Sacramento merchant Shelton C. Fogus. In June 1861, Stanford bought the 4,000 square foot home for $8,000, eventually expanding it to more than 19,000 square feet over the next decade. In 1861 Stanford was elected governor, but his inauguration was dampened by floods that forced him to take a row boat to his inauguration. You can still see the high water marks from the flood in the house. High ceilings, near vertical staircases and ornate, hand-painted wooden walls reveal the age in which Stanford rose to power. Crystal chandeliers, gilded mirrors, impossibly heavy and ornate drapes, French-polished wood paneling and original Stanford family chairs, beds and tables reveal the family's enormous wealth. A billiards table, without side pockets as was the custom of the day, sits in a game room (his wife Jane played) and pianos and other instruments show the family had a musical bent. Especially touching are the photos of the couple's only son Leland Jr. who died at age 15 of typhoid fever while on a family vacation in Europe in 1884. Extremely intelligent (he could speak four languages at an early age) Leland Jr. was headed for Harvard and certainly an outstanding career. His parents mourned him their entire lives, and with a $30 million endowment they founded Leland Stanford Junior College (still the official name of Stanford University) in their son's honor.

Stanford put subtle hints of his railroad days throughout the house; see if you can recognize the cowcatcher, train headlamp and stack on a tall wooden bureau, and find the furniture legs that resemble train engines. Serving just one two-year term as governor, the Stanfords moved out in 1863 and let new Republican Governor Frederick Low, his wife Molly and five year old daughter Flora move in. Stanford felt the state needed a fitting gubernatorial mansion. In an act of bipartisanship that would stun the nation today, Stanford later rented the mansion to Democrat Henry Haight ensuring California's governor could entertain in appropriate fashion no matter which party was temporarily in power. No one is sure where the family lived while other governors trod the floors, but the Stanfords expanded and enhanced the house and re-opened the place in 1872 with a party for 700 guests. With the transcontinental railroad open the Stanfords entertained the high and mighty of the Eastern Establishment who took the rails west to "discover" California. No word on how many stayed rather than return to the blizzards of Philadelphia and New York. Joining other Big Four members, the Stanfords left Sacramento for the cooler weather and hotter social scene of San Francisco's Nob Hill in 1874. But the mansion remained and would live several more useful lives. In 1900 Jane Stanford gave it to the Catholic Bishop of Sacramento and the Sisters of Mercy. It was the sisters who had tenderly cared for young Leland when he died, and Jane Stanford's gift helped other children for the better part of a century. Since California has no official governor's residence (Arnold Schwarzenegger lived in a hotel room during his term while his wife and kids stayed home in Los Angeles) the Stanford mansion serves as the official residence of the state of California and is used to welcome foreign dignitaries. A desk, computer and phone sit in a tiny room hidden in the back, ready for use if a sitting governor needs to spring to action.

WHERE THE SIERRA NEVADA "BEGIN"

Elevation 25 feet

Directions:
Arcade Creek at Haggin Oaks Municipal Golf Course, north side of the clubhouse 3645 Fulton Ave, Sacramento. This is 8.5 miles from Old Sacramento: Take highway 160/I-80 east, and take the Fulton Ave. exit.

Haggin Oaks is one of Sacramento's oldest and most renowned golf courses, with lovely Arcade Creek highlighting the course layout. But before the first club struck a dimpled ball, the land there claimed a spot in history and railroad lore. Arcade Creek became a focal point of the Central Pacific Railroad and even acquired national fame. To build a railway through the mountains was more difficult and expensive than over the flat Sacramento Valley. Charles Crocker, the Central Pacific's construction chief, took the first state geologist, Josiah Whitney, for a ride along Arcade Creek. It was here seven miles from the Sacramento River that Crocker showed him surveyor Theodore Judah's maps which showed land starting to rise toward the distant peaks of the Sierra Nevada. Crocker asked Whitney where the beginning of the mountains should be located. Whitney replied, "Well, the true base [of the Sierra Nevada] is the Sacramento River [7 miles to the west] but for the purpose of this bill, Arcade Creek is as fair a place as any." President Abraham Lincoln agreed, and the Central Pacific would receive $16,000 for each mile built in the valley and $48,000 for each mile of the estimated 150 miles of rugged mountain terrain. With the "mountains" moved 15 miles west, the Central Pacific would receive an additional $240,000 in government bonds, money desperately needed to pay for the railroad's mounting expenses. Walk the course and look to the east. You can feel the ground rise gently toward the mountains. The plaque here reads:

> "On January 12, 1864, President Abraham Lincoln decreed that the western base of the Sierra Nevada began where the Central Pacific Railroad crossed Arcade Creek. The hardships of railroad construction through mountains resulted in increased government subsidies that gave the company impetus to finish the transcontinental railroad."

Before his presidency, Lincoln had represented railroads in a number of important legal cases, and would continue to be a staunch supporter of the transcontinental railroad.

OK... SO JUST CALL IT... THE MOUNTAINS?

How did the Sierra Nevada get its name, and what does it mean?

In 1542, explorer Juan Rodríguez Cabrillo gave the Sierra Nevada its name, which is translated to "snowy range" or "Snowy Mountain" in Spanish. I suppose since then the name has been mangled, twisted and wrought into all kinds of incorrect usage, "the Sierra's" and "the Sierra Nevada's" being the two most common corruptions.

Sierra in Spanish originally referred to a saw. Over time, the name for the jagged blade of a saw evolved metaphorically to be the name for a mountain range with a jagged line of peaks or ragged profile. That's a perfect description of the Sierra Nevada, and sounds much more poetic in Spanish.

Nevada means "snow-covered" in Spanish. I think people who say "Sierra Nevada's" believe they are using it in the plural, not the possessive.

Same with using "The Sierras or Sierra's." Saying "the Sierra Nevada Mountains" seems redundant, since it would translate roughly into "the snow-covered mountain mountains." While it is a massive range, running 400 miles north to south, it is just ONE mountain range.

It would have been easier if Juan, like many explorers, had just named it after himself, but somehow saying "I'm going skiing in the Sierra Cabrillo this weekend" doesn't have the same majestic ring to it. Good call, Juan. ¡Ven a la sierra conmigo!

ROSEVILLE'S GIGANTIC RAILYARD

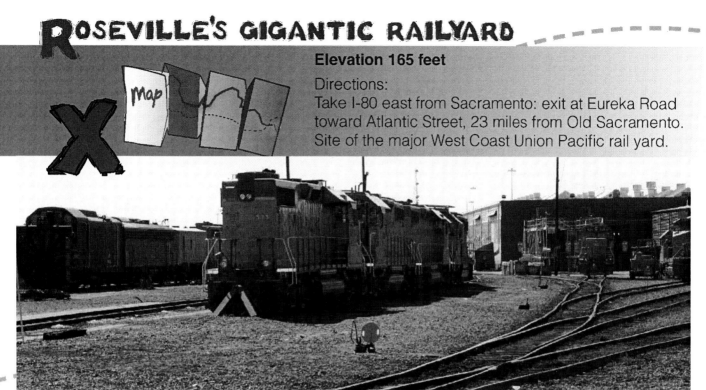

Elevation 165 feet

Directions:
Take I-80 east from Sacramento: exit at Eureka Road toward Atlantic Street, 23 miles from Old Sacramento. Site of the major West Coast Union Pacific rail yard.

If you love watching the big trains rumble, be prepared to take some time in Roseville. Today Roseville is known as a major West Coast rail town, but the city (now numbering about 118,000 souls, with corporations like Hewlett Packard as major employers) originally seemed destined for obscurity. The Central Pacific track layers arrived in 1864 at a small rail line (the California Central Railroad) that linked the young towns of Lincoln and Folsom. They gave the spot the imaginative name of Junction. The town seemed destined to linger as a small way station after the managers of the Central Pacific Railroad picked Rocklin, a few miles east of Roseville, as the spot for central

operations and a large roundhouse. The railroad stayed in Rocklin until 1906, when it ran out of room and shifted operations to Roseville. Today the Union Pacific rail yard has grown to become the largest rail facility on the West Coast. Heading into downtown Roseville on Atlantic Street you soon have

Rails, Tales and Trails

evidence you are in a big rail town. You will see the rail line widen as you approach the gigantic yard. On the right hand side you will see steam engine No. 2252, one of the few remaining T1-class locomotives. The train sits on a small grassy park in front of the rail yard. Stroll over to the impressive 70-ton locomotive and you will get a nice view of the yard and Central Roseville. You can walk down shaded streets on Vernon Street, and stop to visit the folks at Railroad Hobbies. They have a large selection of model trains and railroad merchandise.

Navigating Roseville can be quite a task, as there are 86 miles of track to work around. The yard sits in the middle of Central Roseville and Historic Old Town. Figuring out where you are going can be a tad confusing, but the street signage is good. **To get to Old Town from Vernon Street take the Washington Street underpass and follow the signs.** Old Town Roseville has a historic water tower and solid brick buildings dating back to the 1870s. It is nice and quiet in the day with a pleasant, free observation platform that sits right next to the tracks. You can watch the massive UP trains work their way into the yard from the east, and on a clear day you can see the snow-capped mountains in the distance. A nice railroad-themed restaurant, the **Pacific Street Café, borders the railyard in Old Town at 301 Lincoln Street.** The menu features good food and large helpings at an affordable price, but get there before it closes for the evening at 4PM. At night the streets are populated by the younger nightlife crowd which frequents local establishments like the Boxing Donkey Irish Pub.

A short walk of a block or so from Old Town is the Roseville Amtrak station. Like the depots in Colfax, Auburn and Rocklin, it is a replica of the early CPRR stations. The Roseville depot is operated by a cab company. Passengers wait for trains outside. The depot has some interesting railroad murals on the walls, but no coffee or gift shop, a sad state of affairs for such a famous train town.

Real train buffs will be happy to know that you can circumnavigate the 915-acre Union Pacific rail yard by car. Following Vernon Street from Central Roseville will take you past the main body of the yard. When you reach Cirby Way, take a right and take the next right on Foothills Blvd. Here is a long overpass that affords a wide view of the rail yard. The overpass has a very nice pedestrian sidewalk, so if you want to watch train operations for a while that is the way to get the best view. There is a lot going on all the time, with 247 switches and 2 main lines feeding the 6,500 rail-car capacity yard and a large repair facility. There are a total of 8 receiving and departure tracks, where you can see the trains being built. Something is moving 24-7 in the Roseville yard.

You also might want to explore the residential neighborhoods near Central and Old Roseville. The neighborhoods feature many older craftsman-style homes on well-maintained lawns. Local legend has it that some of these homes were partly built with wood collected from train wrecks back when cabooses and cars were made of wood.

Roseville offers the Galleria, a large and beautiful shopping mall, the Fountains outdoor mall, and many terrific restaurants and nightclubs. These are located a few miles east of Central and Old Roseville, and can easily take up any time or money left after your rail excursion. To some moderns and recent arrivals, the yard is something of a noisy annoyance, and there are complaints of dust and pollution. But for many, Roseville will always be a rail town. At its peak, the railroad employed an estimated 10,000 workers in the 1950s, in 2011 just over 1,100. "When I was a boy growing up in Roseville, everyone worked for the railroad," said former Mayor William M. Santucci. "To me it was a godsend. My dad retired from the railroad, I had two uncles who retired from the railroad. I worked for Southern Pacific when I was going through high school in the summertime, and all my friends did too. If there weren't the railroad and the Pacific Fruit Express, there would not be a Roseville."

So that's why we have ski resorts!

As any old-timer in almost any endeavor will tell you, life in the old days was always just a bit tougher, and the younger generation has it a lot easier. Since 1906, generations of Roseville residents grew up with the railroad which was the major employer in the region. One can hear many memories and stories of life on the rails in the early days, the teller often mixing fact with a few tall tales.

Rail Tales: In 1955 The Roseville Press Tribune interviewed 84-year-old Rudolph E. Noble, a retired engineer who was born at 9th and K Streets in Sacramento, to record his memories of the old days. He had started work with the Southern Pacific in the Sacramento machine shops in 1884 when he was just 15 years old at the sum of $1.25 a day. Nobel piloted a switch engine for awhile and in 1894 he was promoted to engineer and was "on the road" taking trains across the "big hump," as the Sierra Nevada was known to the old railroaders. The first engine driven by Noble was a steam wood-burner, with average speed across the mountains of 10-to-12 miles per hour. He saw the transition from wood burners to coal burners in about 1900 and finally to the diesel-powered engines used today.

He had a unique, if unproven, theory about the region's climate. The trip "over the hill" was much more rugged prior to 1906, he said, not only because of the unrefined equipment, but because of an unusual weather phenomenon. He said that before the San Francisco earthquake of 1906, it never rained above 4,500-foot elevation, and thus there were no rain showers to help melt the snow, which apparently stacked up to prodigious heights and blocked the train's progress. After the quake, according to the ancient trainman, wintertime rains

Rails, Tales and Trails

began to fall in the higher elevations of the Sierra Nevada, melting the snowpack and making it easier for the trains to get through. Before that every trip across the mountains was a battle between engineers and the winter snows, he said. As with thousands of railroad workers for more than a century, he lived the American middle-class dream; he bought a house, proudly became one of the early members of the Brotherhood of Locomotive Engineers and retired in 1937. He told the snow story to the newspaper in 1955 at age 86. He prospered through two world wars, the Great Depression, and countless booms and busts. I have read many accounts of boiler operators, foremen, engineers, and conductors who served more than 50 years, all saying they found railroad work rewarding. I have interviewed engineers who beam with pride as they continue the tradition of taking the big trains over the big bump, battling the elements to keep the products flowing from California to the east. Nobel died at age 98, and I reckon he passed away peacefully. But I'm going to listen closely to the sounds in the High Sierra during winter snowstorms along the rails for the voice of an old engineer guiding his train through a blizzard.

ROCKLIN ROUNDHOUSE
Elevation 248 feet

Directions:
Take I-80 east from Roseville and exit at Rocklin Road.
Take a left on Rocklin road to the railroad tracks. Park in the Amtrak station lot or on the street near Crossroads Church. About 25 miles from Old Sacramento.

Site of the Central Pacific's first-ever roundhouse.

Railroad history favored and then frowned on Rocklin. The original Central Pacific managers decided to build a roundhouse at Rocklin close to the point where the rail bed steepens as it heads toward the foothills. The roundhouse opened in May 1867. It included 25 engine stalls, a turntable and an 8,000 square foot woodshed. The roundhouse's foundation and exterior walls were constructed of rock and masonry, and you can still trace the contours of the roundhouse and see the large rocks from the original building. There is a well-maintained plaque between the church parking lot and the street that marks the roundhouse location. It reads:

> "Central Pacific reached Rocklin, 22 miles from its Sacramento Terminus, in May, 1864, when the railroad established a major locomotive terminal here. Trains moving over the Sierra were generally cut in two sections at this point, in order to ascend the grade. The first CP freight movement was three carloads of Rocklin granite pulled by the engine Governor Stanford."

You will see several sturdy rock buildings, including perhaps the most impressive outhouse ever, made almost entirely of granite. Rocklin is famous for its granite quarries, and supplied

Rails, Tales and Trails

stone for California's state capitol building, the Bank of America, the United States Mint in San Francisco and many other famous civic buildings. A few blocks from the roundhouse remains on Rocklin Road is the granite-clad Rocklin Civic Center. In front of the building is a granite post with holes drilled in it. In the back of the civic center is a small park, and next to it a rather large granite quarry. It was from Rocklin's quarries that the rock for the Central Pacific's first shipment of three carloads of granite was taken. Enjoy the park adjacent to the quarry, so spend some time, look into the quarry and imagine the days when workers bustled and strained to mine the granite and ship it all over the country.

Rocklin's roundhouse was in service continually until 1905 when railroad management announced a major expansion in Roseville. That set off a Rocklin exodus, and many moved their families, belongings and even houses to Roseville. By April 1908 the railroad had moved all roundhouse operations to Roseville and the Rocklin facility closed permanently. Today Rocklin is a major Sacramento suburb offering all the finer amenities.

ROCKLIN TO NEWCASTLE

Elevation 945 feet

Directions: I-80 east to Newcastle exit

You will notice the terrain steadily rising as you head east on Interstate 80. Irregular hills pop up, as if a giant had burrowed underground and punched skyward. You are entering the foot-hills of the Sierra Nevada. If you get a chance, get off the Interstate and drive along Auburn-Folsom Road. It is a busy two-lane road that winds through thriving horse country. Get lost on some of the quiet side roads, or stop off in Loomis, just east of Rocklin. The town was once a major fruit shipper and the Blue Goose fruit packing shed (it has a large blue roof) on Taylor Road offers locally-grown, fresh produce. Grape vines climb the sides of the gently-sloping hills, with a few picturesque wineries tucked here and there. A trip up a ridge can reveal spectacular views, and you can catch stunning vistas of the immense "sugarloaf" crests of the Sierra Nevada on clear days.

A few miles further east is the town of Newcastle, made famous originally by the giant wood trestle the Central Pacific built here in 1864 to cross a large gulch. **Take the Newcastle exit off I-80, cross over the freeway and head into the tiny downtown.** You will see a line of old metal sheds and behind them a crumbling parking lot. You are now driving on the original grade. The parking lot sits on a ledge that overlooks Interstate 80. Drive to the east end of the lot, near the railroad tracks. As you look across the Interstate you will see giant white rocks on the embankment on the other side of the highway. This is where the Newcastle Trestle crossed the ravine. The route was realigned in 1909, and today's trains run on the double-track modern trestle over the freeway and through the tunnel, making this is a great train-watching spot.

Rails, Tales and Trails

According to the marker here, "regular freight and passenger trains began operating over the first 31 miles of Central Pacific's line to Newcastle June 10, 1864, [the marker is in error the actual date was June 6] when political opposition and lack of money stopped further construction during that mild winter. Construction was resumed in April, 1865."

Step back in time and visit Newcastle Produce located just past Newcastle Mini Storage at 9230 Cypress Street. This store is owned by a farming family that has worked the land for seven generations, proud of the produce they sent to market. "We opened Newcastle Produce to share our passion and pride for farming with you. We strive to be your best source for locally grown, farm fresh produce, specialty foods, gourmet meals to go, and more." Stop by and chat and enjoy the fresh foothill food.

A true treasure in Newscastle is Chris Graves, one of a cadre of researchers and historians who live along the old iron route. Chris has assisted many authors, photographers and television producers (including the author) in writing and producing their books, movies and television shows. Chris has spent years hiking and exploring the Central Pacific sites, the old tunnels and abandoned grade. His home, lawns and a large shed in his backyard are a mini-museum of western art and memorabilia. In his travels he has found and preserved many artifacts, including Chinese pottery, old telegraph lines, CPRR payrolls, work rosters and other documents, as well as segments of the original rail laid by the Central Pacific.

Chris is an enthusiastic host and guide, and if you shoot him an email at **caliron@att.net** you will get a reply and may be invited to stop by and see one of the most interesting collections of Western memorabilia you will encounter anywhere.

Also in the Newcastle area you will find large sections of the old rail bed hidden by trees and thick foliage. Since the trains could only handle a gentle grade of two percent, the rail bed trail affords the hiker an easy walk past orchards and ranches. The area is comprised of gently rolling hills, with homes and ranches nestled in the nooks. The original rail beds are twelve-feet wide. While vegetation has grown around it, much of the original rail bed can still be seen. Instead of going over or through hillsides, the surveyors plotted a path that wound around the hills, so the rail bed has wide, gracefully sweeping turns. These beds are not easy to find. Although often within a few hundred feet of the modern line, the original rail bed is usually behind closed fences off of quiet country roads. There are no markers to commemorate the trail. There are a number of clues to tell you if you are on an old rail bed. Ballast—consisting of small stones and rocks—lines the pathway. And you can see the marks where the workers' shovels turned earth and rock to make way for the rails.

Rails, Tales and Trails

AUBURN DAM OVERLOOK

Head back to I-80 if you are in a hurry and continue east and you will arrive in Auburn in less than five minutes. Or if you can, linger, and head south on Indian Hill Road to Auburn Folsom Road, which bends east and takes you to Auburn the slow, scenic way. If you do take Auburn Folsom Road, watch for the signs that say "Auburn Dam Overlook." You won't be looking over a dam, it was never built, but you will be in for some stunning scenery. **Follow Auburn-Folsom Road to Pacific Avenue. Turn right. Go about 0.8 miles to the American River Canyon Overlook, which is on your right.** The Overlook Park offers a beautiful view of the canyon. The park also has access to walking trails and the American River Canyon.

IMAGE MAKER OF THE CENTRAL PACIFIC

We will now be entering some of the most scenic locations along the route and you will want to be sure to have your camera ready. You may recognize some of the scenery from old images in history books, so let's pause and find out how these pictures came to exist. The Central Pacific Railroad used a number of public relations strategies to cultivate good will with opinion makers, potential investors, and the press. Journalists and prominent citizens were given special excursions to the rail head during construction to see the work in progress. For those back east, pictures would be a valuable aid in showing that progress was being made. Collis Huntington, working out of a New York City office, used the pictures to convince investors that their hard-earned money would be wisely invested in railroad bonds. It all helped convince people that the seemingly impossible task of constructing the road over the Sierra Nevada was in fact being accomplished. The man who forged indelible images of the Central Pacific Railroad was Alfred Hart, an artist and portrait photographer hired by Edwin Crocker. Many famous photos in this book and other publications are Hart's work. He was given full access to the construction for three years, and produced 364 photos, or "stereoviews" (an early version of 3D) of the construction in the mountains. His pictures show Chinese laborers, construction foremen, trestles under construction, work in the tunnels and mountains, chugging trains and stunning vistas. He even had a giant mirror hauled high into the mountains to light up the impenetrable darkness inside a massive granite tunnel to make his pictures. Hart had authority to stop trains and halt work crews in order to set up his pictures, but that was one of his few conveniences. As someone who walked in Hart's footsteps, hauled camera gear up steep Sierra slopes, slid down Bloomer Cut and gasped for breath in 6000-foot elevation, I can attest it is no easy task to get to these locations, let alone photograph the dramatic scenes. Hart was working with heavier gear than I was, and an old-fashioned tripod which did not allow him to tilt and swivel the camera head. His painstaking setups and hard work are apparent in the sharp and detailed portraits he produced. He must have had to use all of his powers of persuasion to hold the men, machines and animals in

Rails, Tales and Trails

place for the five seconds it took to make the exposures. Hart did have one advantage over the modern filmmaker: trees along the route had been cleared for construction, offering him many unobstructed vistas that are today blocked by leafy barriers. His pictures will forever remain unique. While Hart's iconic images shaped the very concept of the railroad in the minds of millions of Americans, his work profited him little. After Edwin Crocker died, Hart's relationship with the Central Pacific dissolved. He never held copyright on his art, and as a result his work appeared in many publications, often without attribution, seldom accompanied by payment. As recently as 1989, Hart's photograph "The Monarch from the West" was mistakenly attributed to another photographer. The picture is part of a series that shows the Union Pacific and Central Pacific linking up at Promontory in Utah. The final irony is that the picture was displayed at the Golden Spike National Historic Site Museum, near the spot where Hart made the photograph. Ever the itinerant, Hart lived in Denver, New York and California. He resumed painting, even tried his hand inventing an early version of a movie projector. He lived to age 91, but died a pauper in 1908. His photos will live forever, and can easily be found online, or at the Bancroft Library on the University of California, Berkeley campus, and his Nevada and Utah images at the University of Nevada library in Reno.

AUBURN

Elevations between 1,000 and 1,400 feet
Directions: I-80 exit at Elm Street

Auburn is a beautiful little town tucked right next to the freeway. Its hilly streets offer wonderful vistas, and it is a great town for walking especially if you can catch a glimpse of a train chugging on one of the trestles, knowing they have done this for almost one-hundred and fifty years. If you take the I-80 exit at Elm Street, you will be in Old Town, which dates from the Gold Rush. Old Town took a bit of a hit in 1865 when the Central Pacific reached Auburn and bypassed Old Town and built a depot on a hill about a mile and half away. Most businesses packed up and relocated to the new depot area, leading to two downtowns for this small town. Both offer nice restaurants, antique stores and pleasant hilly hikes. Today you will find a perfect replica of the old depot with offices occupied by the Chamber of Commerce at **601 Lincoln Way.** The railroad did not just disrupt business; it had a huge impact on people, many of whom blamed the railroad for disrupting their quiet, pastoral lives. One of the CPRR's "villains" was big, blustery hard-hearted, one-eyed James Harvey Strobridge. Immortalized over time as the construction boss who browbeat and bullied workers, Strobridge was accused of pushing them past exhaustion to accomplish tasks thought to be impossible. Strobridge has been portrayed as one of the toughest guys in American history, even depicted in one television series engaged in axe-handle battles with

Rails, Tales and Trails

workers to keep them in line. But Strobridge had a softer side. When the railroad reached Auburn in May, 1865 it caused immediate and unbeatable competition for the California Stagecoach Company, which laid off its station manager, Samuel H. Whitmarsh. With two children to support, and no job, Whitmarsh fell into depression and shot himself through the head. The "cruel" Strobridge, in the midst of construction, adopted the boy and the girl. It was at Auburn that the railroad first began to employ Chinese workers in large numbers. They are memorialized with a 22-foot high monument next to the old train depot. It was sculpted by a local dentist and never fails to draw attention from tourists.

A TRUE WONDER, BLOOMER CUT

Directions: End of Herdal Drive, Auburn
From eastbound I-80 take the Maple Street exit in Auburn and stay straight. Go through the stoplight and continue on Auburn Folsom Road. After about 1 ¼ miles, turn right onto Herdal Drive. Park where Herdal Drive ends at Quinn Way and take the walking trail heading east. Bloomer Cut will be about 300 feet ahead.

The cut was once regarded as the Eighth Wonder of the World. It is located in Auburn in a quiet residential neighborhood, west of downtown. It is a rocky trail that rises and falls so be sure to wear hiking shoes. You can climb to the top of the cut and peer down the vertical side and see the railroad tracks.

It was one of the first engineering challenges the railroad faced. On February 22, 1864, workers began the dangerous and exhausting job of cutting a wedge through a tough, rocky hill. The hill was described as consisting of "boulders embedded in cement." Look at it today and you can see how the cut sides of the hill have withstood the vagaries of time with very little erosion. The cut is an engineering marvel and a testament to the strength and determination of the laborers who built it. The workers used black powder to blast through the hill— building a tunnel without a top. The cut is 800 feet long, and the workers excavated more than 45,000 cubic yards of earth and rock, using shovels, picks and wagons. The work could be dangerous, as evidenced by what occurred to the project's hands-on construction chief, James Harvey Strobridge. He was working in the cut when a powder charge went off; his injury cost him the use of an eye. Strobridge was back at work the next day.

You can still see the marks from pick and shovel. The railroad still runs on the original route today, and trains barely squeeze through the narrow passage.

Rails, Tales and Trails

BAYLEY HOUSE

Directions:

From Auburn Take Highway 49 south and east about 6.7 miles past the town of Cool This is a 20-minute drive down a winding road featuring hairpin turns, over the American River and through the beautiful Auburn State Recreation Area. Stop by the river and look around, you will notice the Foresthill Bridge, at 731 feet above the riverbed the fourth highest bridge in the U.S. There are also some nice, short hikes along the river. Continue on Highway 49 and you will come to a three-story brick building, standing all alone, on the right-hand side of the road.

Like just about everybody and their proverbial brother, businessman A.J. Bayley wanted a piece of the speculative action the railroad offered. He believed the rail route would follow a well-known wagon freight route, so he built a grand 22-room hotel alongside what he thought would be the railroad. Visions of dusty tourists getting off the train and paying top dollar for a respite at his hotel jumped in his head. Those hopes were dashed when Theodore Judah put the road on the other side of the canyon you just drove through. Bayley finished his "hotel" using 300,000 bricks, which a local writer said made it stand out "like the veritable sore thumb." Its doors opened in April 1862, but with no train traffic its commercial future was doomed, so Bayley lived there. Bayley survived the debacle and built the Grand Central Hotel and Resort near Truckee this time along a thriving tourist rail line, so his concept played out if the timing did not. Unfortunately the Bayley House is boarded up so you won't be able to see the ornate wooden staircases and other affectations of 1850s-era wealth, and over time the scoffers dubbed it "Bayley's Folly."

Here you may enjoy a wonderful drive, spectacular scenery, and can forever tell friends you were in Cool, California. You can even make up a catchy story about how Cool got its name, since no one really knows.

Rails, Tales and Trails

CLIPPER GAP

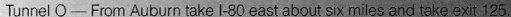

Elevation 1676 feet

Directions:
Tunnel O — From Auburn take I-80 east about six miles and take exit 125.

Take a right turn off the freeway and an immediate left on Applegate. Head east on eight-tenths of a mile to Fairidge (that's how the road is spelled) and turn right. Cross the bridge over the small creek and park your vehicle off the main road, walk down the dirt road to a chain that blocks vehicle traffic. Continue on that road about 1/4 mile, at which time you will see the shore of the lake on your right. Continue on that road until you come to a steep hill, at that junction you will walk to the East, up a slight incline. At the top of that incline, you will be walking on old CPRR grade. Continue walking East, you will soon come to LIVE RAILS. Tunnel "0" is about 1/2 mile in front of you, behind a large oak tree. Here, just off the modern track and hidden behind a few bushes is tunnel "O." Tunnel "O" is east of Clipper Gap. It is 711 feet long, bored through Wildcat Summit between Clipper Gap and Applegate, this to eliminate the 90-foot-high trestle at Deep Gulch. It can be hard to find the entrance to the 711 foot-long tunnel since it's obscured by trees and brush. The structure is shaped like a horseshoe with sides that taper inward near the bottom. Because of its proximity to the Union Pacific tracks, and more than a mile by foot from the Clipper Gap exit off Interstate 80, visitors should check with the railroad's Roseville office on rules about traveling on or near the right of way. This unique tunnel was opened to rail traffic on July 24, 1873 and served until WWII when it was abandoned because boats and landing craft used by the military were too wide to fit through the tapered tunnel.

COLFAX

Elevation 2400 feet

Directions: Take I-80 east from Auburn 17 miles and take Exit 135 toward Colfax.

A twenty minute drive up I-80 from Auburn brings you to Colfax, a quiet, quaint town, above the fog of the valley and just below where the Sierra can deal a devastating snow storm. Many of the downtown buildings date back to the early railroad days. Browse Main Street and read the plaques on the stores that tell the story. It's easy to stroll from the downtown area to the modern Amtrak station, where passengers board the train for the start of the journey through the higher elevations. Visit the old train depot and see the baggage carts and travel cases that are reminders of the heyday of rail passenger service. Here the visitor information center can give you detailed information on walking to several sites that housed railroad operations. Check out the vintage railroad pictures and old maps in the quaint Colfax Area Historical Society also in the depot. Look at some of the old photos of Colfax there. You will notice that the hills are denuded. Look at the hills today. Lush, green, 150 year old trees dominate the landscape. The trees had been chopped down to provide firewood for the old wood-burning steam engines. Oil replaced steam, made the trains faster, and saved the trees.

Original Grade.

You can see a prime example of original constructiongoing east on Hwy. 174. **Go about eight-tenths of a mile from the Red Frog and turn right on Norton Grade Road. At 1.8 miles stay on Norton Grade as it bends to the right. At 3.6 miles turn right under the freeway overpass onto Cape Horn Road. You will notice hillocks on either side of your vehicle-these are the fills created by the workers. You are actually riding on the rail bed. At 5.9 miles you will see a short path on the left side and a gate past it. Park here. Follow the curving path and you will get a real feel for how the grade wrapped around the mountains.**

A great spot for a meal is TJ's Roadhouse, offering good, affordable and plentiful food. Make sure you try the home-made potato chips and always check for what new dessert is on the menu. It's a nice and relaxed spot frequented by locals and you can enjoy beer or wine after a hot day on the trail. Once called Illinoistown, the town is named after Schuyler Colfax, once Speaker of the U.S. House of Representatives. Colfax was a true politician of the genial, back-slapping variety and earned the nickname of "Smiler" Colfax. Today his statue sits near the train depot and is usually ignored by the busy passengers. Through the years, the telling of the story on how the town was renamed has come to be a tale of the slippery ways the Big Four had of influencing politicians.

Like Lincoln, Colfax was a long-time supporter of a transcontinental railroad. Colfax was Republican Speaker of the House during much the Civil War, and thus at the center of sweeping historical events and a key figure in the Union victory and abolishing slavery. Lincoln's famous Emancipation Proclamation was a wartime declaration, not a law. In order to form a firm legal basis to abolish slavery, the Thirteenth Amendment to the Constitution had to be passed by Congress. This was hardly a done deal and had stalled in the House, a few votes short of the two-thirds majority required to pass the House Chamber. By January, 1865 it became apparent the Union was going to win the war, so pressure mounted to make sure slavery was forever abolished. Working closely with Lincoln, Colfax cut deals to bring the reluctant House members into line; one was offered a government job for his brother, another offered support to hold onto his seat. As soon as the vote was sewn up, Colfax brought the

Rails, Tales and Trails

measure to the floor and it was passed with just three changed votes to spare. Wild cheering broke out in Congress and the streets of Washington, with the amiable Colfax no doubt leading the celebration.

Colfax was one of the last people to talk to Lincoln. As his carriage waited to take him to the fateful play at Ford's theatre, Colfax met briefly with the President to get final approval for a journey to the west coast. After speaking at several of the large observances that honored Lincoln after his death, Colfax embarked on his trip, designed partly to visit the Central Pacific Railroad. Word of the tour spread and in July, while Speaker Colfax was arriving in Sacramento, Leland Stanford, president of the CPRR, changed the name of the town, making it Colfax officially July 29, 1865. The reason, cynics said, was to get favors from the railroad from the powerful politician, obscuring Colfax's impressive contributions to the nation during its greatest crisis. Stanford had served as California's Republican Governor in 1862 and 63, winning on a pro-Lincoln, anti-slavery platform. It seems likely Stanford's action in naming the town was to honor a man he greatly admired.

What did Colfax see on his trip? We can't be sure, but Samuel Bowles, traveling part of the time with Colfax, reported in his journal, *Across the Continent* (1865) "Our party made a very profitable and interesting excursion over the route of the Central Pacific Road from Sacramento to Donner Lake, on the eastern slope of the mountains, by special train and coaches, and along the working sections on horseback. The track is graded and laid, and trains are running to the new town of Colfax (named for the Speaker), which is fifty-six miles from Sacramento. Grading is now in active progress on the next section, to Dutch Flat."

The Central Pacific reached the town in September, 1865, and it turned into an anthill of activity as the railroad paused to organize for the heavy weather and heavier construction that lay ahead as the elevation steadily increased.

TRUTH AND LEGEND OF CAPE HORN AND THE CHINESE WORKERS

Elevation 2,654 feet

Directions: Take Highway 174 2.5 miles from Colfax to Cape Horn

Cape Horn is a high rocky promontory that offers spectacular views of the American River Canyon. You can view Cape Horn from the Red Frog bar on Highway 174, about half a mile north of Colfax. The Cape Room in the back offers spectacular views. It's best to bring

binoculars for a close look. From the Red Frog you can see the wide, curving sweep the railroad engineers carved around the steep peninsula high above the American River Canyon.

Cape Horn was once a name that ranked with the top tourist destinations in California. I have one of those old-fashioned maps of California dating from around 1900 that are crammed with facts and illustrations of the top scenic wonders. Highlighted along with Yosemite and the Giant Redwoods is Cape Horn. It gained its fame when eastern tourists began to take the train ride west in the 1870s.

They had read tour guides which promoted the spectacular scenery they would see from the train as they traveled through the mountains. But in order to operate during the snowy winters, the railroad had covered forty miles of track in the upper elevations with wooden snow sheds, completely obstructing the view for train passengers, who felt like they were riding through a dark barn. It wasn't until the lower elevations that the sheds were not needed. Cape Horn was one of the first spots with a clear view of mountain scenery. The trains would stop at Cape Horn and tourists would get out and walk to the side of the hill for a first peek at scenic California. The CPRR publicists promoted the story of Cape Horn, and tour books, some subsidized by the railroad, spread the story far and wide. It became known throughout the nation as a "must see" spot not to be missed.

Rails, Tales and Trails

A durable legend (unfortunately published in some best-selling books about the railroad) claimed that Chinese workers were suspended over the side of the mountain in wicker bosuns' chairs. The legend said that the workers had to hang over the side in baskets in order to bore holes into the mountain to hold black powder, then ignite the powder and blast off chunks of the slope. Claims were made that 300 Chinese lost their lives in the effort, and the plaque in the parking lot of the Red Frog reads:

> "Dedicated to the memory of thousands of Chinese who worked for Charles Crocker on the Central Pacific Railroad. They were lowered over the face of Cape Horn Promontory in wicker Bosun's chairs to a point 1332 feet above the canyon floor. The ledge created for the railbed was completed May 1866. They are honored for their work ethic, and timely completion of the Transcontinental Rails ending in Promotory, [SIC] Utah, May 1869."

Two excellent short books have been written on Cape Horn, books which celebrated authors did not consult when repeating or creating the wicker basket myth. *A Study of Cape Horn Construction on the Central Pacific Railroad 1865-1866* by Jack E. Duncan, an engineer, presents detailed charts and measurements that show how impractical the hanging basket myth is. *The Central Pacific Railroad and the Legend of Cape Horn 1865-1866* traces the myth. That book is written by Edson T. Strobridge, a descendent of James Harvey Strobridge, the CPRR's Superintendent of Construction. You might find these books in Colfax at the gift store in the train depot. Walking the route and examining the evidence, you will see that it is NOT a sheer drop to the canyon floor. The American River is visible, but not immediately below the cape. Indeed, you could not hang off the side by a rope if you wanted to — the slope is not that steep. The rock itself is not the granite found in higher elevations but a softer, metamorphic fissile surface that is fairly easy to cut through. There were no newspaper stories or other accounts of Chinese hanging over the side at Cape Horn. What did happen, it appears, is that imaginative railroad public relations writers later spun a story for the entertainment of tourists. That story was repeated in several best-selling books about the transcontinental railroad over the years, perpetuating the myth of the wicker baskets.

Cape Horn construction took three months. It is rumored that Chinese artifacts, dating back to 1865, are still found at the base of Cape Horn by amateur archaeologists and hikers. Note, I have never found any! **To walk under the promontory, take the North Canyon Way exit 135, travel along North Canyon Way past the Colfax cemetery to the Stevens trailhead and find the parking area on Canyon Way.** The 4.5 mile trail was originally used as a toll road from Colfax down to Secret Ravine along the American River, and then to Iowa Hill which was a Gold Rush boomtown. When the gold played out the miners left and the road was all but forgotten until 1969 when, the BLM says "a Sacramento-area Boy Scout was credited with rediscovering the trail." You will get spectacular views of the steep American River North

Rails, Tales and Trails

Fork Canyon. "During the months of April and May, you will be treated to a beautiful wildflower display. Dogwoods and redbud represent the larger flowering plants, while baby blue eyes, shooting stars, monkey flowers, lupines and tiger lilly brighten the lower plant canopies," says the BLM trail guide. On the hike you will pass under the Cape Horn promontory and you can see the trains rounding the Cape above you. You will also pass several mine shafts, and other Gold Rush era sites. The kind folks at the BLM warn visitors to steer clear of the mines, which are unstable and extremely dangerous.

You can make a day of exploring for gold, railroad artifacts and scenery in one of California's most intriguing spots.

Elevation 2,904 feet

Directions:
Take 80 east five miles from Colfax and take the Secret Town exit.

SECRET TOWN

1100 feet long and 100 feet high, the Secret Town trestle is famous today due to the photo here (next page) showing Chinese workers moving earth with small carts. The wooden trestle was built in 1866, but the photo not taken until 1876. In its race to build the route quickly, the trestles were not filled in with earth until years later. As you drive west, the earthen trestle will loom up on a curve. Looking up, you can see how enormous the structure was.

Secret Town Trestle.

Also at Secret Town, hidden off the old grade at the bottom of a ravine with its entrance obscured, is a small stone structure that puzzled local historians for years. Many conjectured it was a workingman's emergency shelter, a compact bordello, a Chinese religious shrine or an opium den. At just 6 feet in diameter and four and a half feet from floor to ceiling, debate raged as to exactly what it could have been used for. The answer (as is many times the case) proved to be nothing nefarious. According to Priscilla Wegars of the University of Idaho, the tiny stone structures can be found along railroad grades throughout the west and were used as baking ovens by Greek and Italian workers. No one has fired it up recently, but I bet it made delicious bread, and maybe even pizza?

Finding the oven takes some work, but here is how to get there: From the Secret Town exit off 80 headed east, at the end of the off ramp turn left, drive back over the freeway, and turn right on Secret Town Road.

Rails, Tales and Trails

You are now driving parallel to the freeway, driving east, about one mile. In front of you, you will see the bridge the cars take over the rails; as you approach the rails, there is a wee track that goes to the left. Take that dirt road, and continue going east, driving parallel to the rails. Proceed 100 yards, the road bears off to the left a bit, and goes through a cut. The rails continue to be on your right, but now a ways off. Go a quarter mile, and the road drops down, but the rails are up, as they continue to be on the old Secret Town trestle as you continue driving. You will come to the end of the trestle, and shortly you will see a dirt track that goes up to the rails. There is a hill in front of you. Go up that road, near the rail line and park. On the other side of the rails is a heavily wooded area and to your left there is a "cut." In front of you there is a steep decline. Go down that decline. Bear to the right a bit. At the bottom of the decline, there is a flat area. Proceed over that flat. There is a sharp drop-off, and at the bottom you will find the oven, built into the side of the hill. It's hard to find but lots of fun looking.

GOLD RUN

Elevation 3,212 feet
Directions:
Take 80 east 1.5 miles from Secret Town.

There is a very clean and well-maintained rest stop here with a large outdoor area to sit and relax. There is an impressive marker in front of the rest rooms that reads: "Chinese Railroad Workers. About 1,000 feet from this location is the track of the transcontinental railroad. In 1865 thousands of Chinese in Kwantung Province China were recruited to work on this great connection between the east and west coast. This monument is dedicated to the memory of those Chinese laborers who worked for Charles Crocker of the Central Pacific Railroad." Inside the men's room are images of Theodore Judah and an image of the construction of the Secret Town Trestle.

In 1859 miners started hydraulic mining here on a bed of gravel two miles long, half a mile wide and 250 feet deep. It yielded more than six million dollars worth of gold, and attracted such a crowd that the place was named Gold Run in 1863.

Rails, Tales and Trails

DUTCH FLAT

Elevation 3.144 feet

Directions:
Continue east on 80 about five miles from Secret Town to the delightful town of Dutch Flat. For a look at early California, this pristine town is not to be missed.

First settled by gold miners, Dutch Flat was an important wagon road, later a center of railroad construction. Floods, fires and commercialism have forever altered many Mother Lode towns, but hilly Dutch Flat transports visitors back to the 1860's. It remains unspoiled, untouched by any type of franchise restaurants, and features biking and hiking trails just steps from downtown.

As the local Golden Drift Historical Society put it, "because Dutch Flat was fortunate never to have suffered from a catastrophic fire, exists close to but not on the transcontinental railroad, and is close to but not on the State Highway [or I-80] many of the old buildings from the 1800s are still standing. Town streets are laid out just as they were in the 1860s, and you can use them to help you imagine what it was like back in the 1800s." Sit on the porch at the Museum with a few of the locals, and you will feel like you are in a New England township rather than California. Next door, flags flying from its three porches rising above Main Street, sits the Dutch Flat Hotel, a picture of Americana. Originally built as a 50-room hotel the classic red clapboard structure trimmed in bright white served as a private residence, vacation home and business office during its storied life. Renovated in the last decade, the hotel was closed

Rails, Tales and Trails

in 2012 but still features a beautiful back terrace and lush lawn. It's for sale now, and may be your chance to own that peaceful bed and breakfast you always wanted. Realtors are standing by. Down a side street is the shining white Methodist Church that provided a place of worship and confession for the hard working, hard drinking 49ers. It was built starting in 1850 and today is as beautiful as ever.

In 1853, Dutch Flat had a population of 6,000, well over half of them Chinese. In 1877 the Chinatown burned down, and the settlement relocated south of town, near the Dutch Flat Depot on the Central Pacific Railroad. Adjoining the pioneer American cemetery just above

the town is the Chinese burial ground. The remains were long ago returned to China, as was the Chinese custom of the time.

You can visit the Chinese exhibit in the Golden Drift Museum, and learn about the town's contributions to the Gold Rush and the Central Pacific Railroad. Run by knowledgeable volunteers in a gingerbread house, hours can vary greatly so contact them ahead of time if you want to make sure you can see it and them. Or just hang out on the porch awhile, somebody usually wanders by.

In October 1860 Theodore Judah, the man who planned the railroad route, met with a druggist who serviced the gold miners, Dutch Flat resident Dr. D.W. Strong. It was here that Strong showed Judah the ridge line that would take the railroad through the mountains and over Donner Summit. Judah and Strong, ahead of the game and without the knowledge of the Big Four in Sacramento, drew up a stock subscription and used the name "Central Pacific Railroad" for the first time. Now Judah would plot a course that took advantage of the tilt of the Sierra Nevada, which provided a relatively gentle gradient up the western slope. As Judah put it in a promotional pamphlet, "Confident of the existence of a practical route across the Sierra Nevada Mountains...I have devoted the past few months to an exploration of several routes and passes through Central California, resulting in the discovery of a practicable route

Rails, Tales and Trails

from the city of Sacramento upon the divide between Bear River and the North Fork of the American, via Illinoistown, Dutch Flat, and Summit Valley to the Truckee River; which gives nearly a direct line to Washoe, Nevada with maximum grades of one hundred feet per mile.

The elevation of the Pass is 6,690 feet." For the next three years the relationship between Judah and his bosses would feature arguing and bickering. The Big Four had plans for a wagon road leading from Dutch Flat and over the mountains into Nevada to charge tolls to shippers doing business with the Nevada silver trade. Central Pacific rivals, abetted by Judah who worried that the wagon road would soak up money and resources that should go to railroad construction, launched a furious public relations war against the railroad.

.The "Dutch Flat Swindle" became nationally infamous with hot copy like this from the Alta, Californian: "The Sacramentans [Big Four] are determined to have no railroad but one ending at Dutch Flat. The Capital City has aided in the raid upon this San Francisco county for $80,000, upon Placer County for $25,000, and upon the state for millions. There will never be a railroad via Dutch Flat to Nevada Territory. There are obstacles which cannot be overcome. The Pacific Railroad will follow another route, not through Sacramento or anywhere else in the vicinity." As noted earlier many San Franciscans never got over the fact that they had passed up the chance to be Judah's original investors.

Judah made threats about finding rich eastern capitalists and wresting control from the Big Four and building the railroad where he wanted it built. But he died of fever in 1863. The railroad promptly hired Judah's former assistant, Samuel S. Montague, as new chief engineer, and he would brilliantly guide the rails through the Sierra Nevada without complaining. He would astonish the critics and finish the task in four years. The wagon road was also built and became a profitable enterprise that served teamsters headed to the Nevada Comstock lode. The wagon road was eventually replaced by Highway 40, and you can still occasionally find wagon wheel ruts on the sides of the road as you travel to the summit.

EARLY ROLLERCOASTER, THE TOWLE BROTHERS RAILROAD

Another company you will encounter in Dutch Flat is the Towle (pronounced Toll) Brothers Lumber Company, which once operated 15 saw mills in Nevada and Placer Counties. They began as pioneer lumbermen of the Dutch Flat area providing lumber for the mines. The Towle Brothers supplied lumber and timber for the snow sheds and trestles for the Central Pacific as it laid track in the high country and over Donner Summit. The company set up its own narrow-gauge railroad to drag logs from the forests to their various sawmills to meet increas-

Rail Tales
The Towles employed so many people they started their own town, but the people, the towns, the trains and the lumber mills are all now gone. The company was sold to a Canadian firm around 1902, and they eventually shut down the railroad. The Towle Brothers rest in the Old Dutch Flat cemetery. There are rumors that some of the old locomotives are hidden in the forest, but the only visible reminder of the busy days gone by is a restored caboose across from the church in Dutch Flat.

ing demand. At their peak in the 1880s the Towle Brothers operated five steam engines. A 35-mile long railroad line connected their mills with the Central Pacific Railroad, and the lumber was transferred for shipping to all parts of the Pacific Coast. They were also pioneers in the manufacturing of wooden fruit boxes from sugar and yellow pine. The company employed approximately 70 Chinese men, who were constantly working on new track and grading for extension of the rail line.

As you will see when you drive or hike around the area, the terrain is steep, and according to a local newspaper account of the era, could have been a model for a future roller coasters: "It is twenty miles long, but an air line of ten miles would cover the distance between its termini... It has no curves; they are all angles. Its "up and down" course is as eccentric as its confused tangle of lateral bends, twists, and convolutions. In one place the grade is over 230 feet to the mile. Starting on a train from Towles, which is only 3,700 feet above the sea, you suddenly find yourself, with a few jerks and tosses into the air, hoisted to an elevation of 5,200 feet, and from this point you are suddenly dropped, with a whirl, a bump, and a crash into the depths of a miniature Yosemite."

The landscape that once featured such wild rides is all quiet now and deeply forested. Original Towle Brothers rail beds can be easily found along Highway 20 on Burlington Ridge and near North Fork Campground on the Texas Hill road. Portions of the Texas Hill road were built on the Towle Brothers' rail bed.

PLACER COUNTY'S – YOSEMITE, GIANT GAP

Elevation 3,800 feet

Directions:
Take I-80 east 1.8 miles from Dutch Flat and exit at Alta.
Exit right (the opposite direction from Alta) and take an immediate left onto Casa Loma Road. At 0.8 the road bends sharply to the right over a one-lane bridge and small canal. Stay on this narrow, winding and beautiful blacktop road for 1.8 miles. You can either stop here and walk to the canyon rim or continue down the dirt road until you see the outhouse. The parking for the Euchre trailhead is there, and you can walk down the road toward the canyon, enjoying many stunning vistas.

This spectacular area has been called "Placer County's Yosemite" which may actually understate the natural beauty found here. The American River cuts a deep gorge through the mountains forming a deep canyon and offers expansive views of wave after wave of

mountains and hills receding in the distance. It is an easy walk from the road to the side of the canyon, and you can easily hike around the rim for different views, all spectacular. There are trails that lead to the bottom of the canyon and the river, and I believe it is possible to four-wheel to the bottom but I have not done that. Kayakers from all over the world come here to run the rapids, and you can see the white water churning from the canyon rim above. There is a light bluish haze in the canyon, gentle mountain breezes and the modern track runs around the canyon rim offering spectacular photo opportunities for the train buff. There are dirt and gravel roads that branch off from Casa Loma Road and they are in good shape, but you would be advised to take a four-wheel vehicle. If you have time, take Moody Ridge Road off Casa Loma and look for the sign that reads "Lovers Leap." You are ascending at a fairly good rate and the road is rutted and no doubt a mess when it rains. The great thing is you will have this sublime experience almost to yourself. That can hardly be said of Yosemite these days.

Like Cape Horn, Giant Gap was once nationally famous and has lapsed into undeserved anonymity. The Central Pacific Railroad reached Alta in 1866 and the huge work force pushed rapidly east along the ridge to Cisco. Some of the first tourists to see the canyon were amazed, and soon the railroad's public relations machine was inspiring stories like this one...

Rails, Tales and Trails

"There suddenly opens on the gaze of the expectant traveler, just before the sunlight has quite disappeared, and the evening shades come on, the vision of The Great American Cañon,–by far the finest cañon of the entire Pacific Railroad. The suddenness of approach and the grandeur of scene are so overpowering, that no pen, picture of language can give it adequate description. Two thousand feet below, flow the quiet waters of the American River. Westward is seen the chasm, where height and peak and summit hang loftily over the little vale." So wrote Thomas Moran in his1876 guidebook, *The Pacific Tourist*.

Dutch Flat writer and historian Russell Towle wrote about the American River Canyon for many years. He explained the importance of Giant Gap in the American psyche. "Americans in the Eastern states had been hearing about the wild and deep canyons of the Sierra for two decades, since the Gold Rush. Sensible folk realized that the 49ers, like other humans, were given to exaggeration; the canyons were not that deep, not that steep, not that wild. But to ride the train into California, to break free of the snowsheds at Blue Canyon, to reach the promontory at Casa Loma, then called Green Bluffs, was to see Giant Gap. And to see Giant Gap was to realize that, if anything, the 49ers had understated the case for Sierran canyons. The guidebooks to California lavished praise upon this view; famed landscape artist Thomas Moran executed a fine etching of Green Valley and Giant Gap; and the awesome scene even inspired a brief effort to rename that amazing gorge Jehovah Gap."

Rail Tales
The railroad built an observation deck, and passengers on the way west would get out, stretch their legs and flip coins over the side for good luck.

The Railroad Ghost Town at Cisco

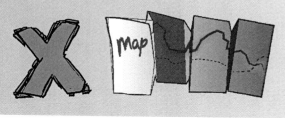

Elevation 5,938 feet

Directions:
Take I-80 20 miles east from Colfax to Cisco. The old town is up the dirt road that goes past the gas station, bear to the right.

There is nothing much to recommend a stop at the Cisco exit these days, just a gas station and a hotel. But it is here that the Central Pacific prepared for the hardest stretch of construction, 28 miles from Cisco to the Truckee River. The railroad would have to figure out how to carve out 15 tunnels through the granite backbone of the Sierra Nevada, a combined length of more than a mile. And it is at this high elevation that the weather became a terrible, unpredictable factor. Winter could begin in September and storms rage into May. Take the rutted dirt road and you will find the remains of a camp that housed more than 10,000 people in 1867. You can see the foundations and splintered timbers, and find iron spikes and nails a few inches under the ground. Walk down the sloping dirt paths that were once busy streets clogged with Chinese and Anglo workers. Stone houses, power houses, blacksmith shops, a kitchen, stables for mules, horses and oxen and small buildings for the workers, all strong enough to survive blizzards, had to be constructed. It made, one observer said, "quite a village."

Rails, Tales and Trails

THE LOST WATCHMAN'S HOUSE ON SIGNAL PEAK ON RED MOUNTAIN

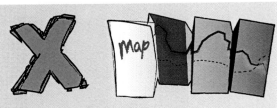

Elevation 7,680 feet

Directions: Headed east take the Cisco Grove exit and turn left, back over the freeway. Turn left (west) on the frontage road, and travel on to the store (about 0.25 mile). In the winter, buy a permit in the store and park in the plowed lot. In summer, Fordyce Lake Road begins slightly before the entry kiosk to the campground, on the north side of the road. The signage will direct you to Woodchuck Flat. If you don't want to drive off-road you can choose to leave your car here and continue on foot. If you have a high clearance vehicle you can press on. Continue on Fordyce Lake Road approximately 1.15 mile to where the trail begins. Make sure to check weather conditions as it can be snowbound through June.

Millions of people pass Red Mountain on I-80 every year and never give it a second look. Getting up it—even in a four wheeler—is not easy. It's a narrow one-lane road clinging to the side of the mountain. You never know who or what you'll meet around the next corner, like the giant logging trucks that make their way ponderously down the mountain. And if they are bigger than you the only option you have is to back down the mountain a bit. The road is very steep. In the first mile and a quarter it rises 900 feet. In total the route is only three and a quarter miles long, but rises 2,100 feet. Up, up it goes. The last few hundred yards are the hardest. Those last yards are like climbing stairs that shift under you. If you are up to challenging hikes though, the walk is a good one if you don't make it too late in the year. Wildflowers, butterflies, streams, and meadows are all nice additions to the gorgeous views. In summer the dirt is dry and the hike is very dusty and hot. Wear boots that support you since there is a lot of loose rock. Bring water.

On Signal Peak you will find a building that served as a fire look-out from 1909 until 1934. Watchmen lived up here, on round-the-clock duty looking for fires along the route, and dispatching emergency help via telegraph. To prevent Donner Summit's heavy snowfall (35 feet a year) from stopping train traffic, the Central Pacific built almost 40 miles of wooden snow sheds. Those snow sheds kept the tracks free of snow, but were also a fire hazard as they baked in the summer sun. Sparks from locomotives set them off and special fire trains were kept ready with full heads of steam to speed off and fight the fires. It is obvious why this was the lookout spot. You will get a spectacular 360-degree view, and from here you can see the miles of railroad line snaking through the mountains. It's the perfect place to relax and marvel at the beauty and complexity of the route. Be sure to bring powerful binoculars for a close-up look at the rail line. On a clear day you can see from the crest of the Sierra Nevada to the west and southwest into the Sacramento Valley and Coast Range, including Mount Diablo. You have a wonderful look at sparkling Lake Spalding, more than 2,500 feet below, sitting just to the west contentedly resting in its glacier-carved bowl of granite.

THE OLD, SLOW AND BEAUTIFUL ROUTE 40

You are now leaving the I-80 corridor and will head south a bit. You will be driving on the Old Lincoln Highway, Route 40, also known as Donner Pass Road.

The Donner Pass Road bends spectacularly above Donner Lake, then rejoins the freeway through Donner Pass. This is an area of extreme change. In this area you will find alpine meadows, glacier-formed lakes, and mountain crests thrust against California's blue skies. Native Americans, wagon masters, and of course the railroad builders all left plenty to see in this region.

Rails, Tales and Trails

BIG BEND IN THE TAHOE NATIONAL FOREST

Elevation 5,700 feet

Directions:
Take the Rainbow or Big Bend exit from I-80 and follow the Ranger Station signs along old U.S. 40.

A great place to stop on your trip is Big Bend in the Tahoe National Forest. Until recently there was a great little museum here, but it has closed. Still it is worth wandering the grounds here in search of history. This is one of the major transportation corridors of the world, a high mountain pass where Native Americans, pioneers, and the railroad found a way through the mountains. In the Big Bend area you will find roadbed and a dozen tunnels carved from some of the hardest granite in the world. You can also find ruts in the granite rocks, carved by the early wagon trains and stage coaches. Picnic in the shade, and if you are so inclined do some serious hiking and mountain scrambling.

Rails, Tales and Trails

PLEASURES OF THE OLD STAGECOACH ROUTE, THE RAINBOW LODGE

Directions: From the east, take Rainbow Road (exit 168) off of I-80. Turn right and follow the road (which is historic Highway 40.) Rainbow Lodge will be on your left.
Note: Rainbow Lodge says its location is not "GPS compatible."

This is my favorite spot for a drink or meal in the Donner Summit area, and I have spent many a happy hour enjoying the historic photos, great conversations and libations in the beautiful lounge and bar. The Yuba River flows over magnificent granite rocks just a few hundred feet from the front door. In spring the river can roar past, while in September, before the snow falls, the river slows to a trickle exposing massive river-bed rock formations. Rainbow Lodge's history dates back to the late 1800s. Those so inclined can walk the grounds framed by its original stone walls. The Lodge was built in the 1880s as a stage coach stop that connected to the Central Pacific. The Lodge became a hit with guests who would travel up the mountain from Sacramento and San Francisco to catch prize rainbow trout in the Yuba. They would bring in their catch of the day and have the Rainbow chef cook it. As the ski industry developed in the early 1900s skiers stopped in and rented equipment for the fast-growing sport. You will enjoy the pictures of early skiers, hikers and tourists that line the wooden walls. Rainbow features water from an artesian spring located deep in the granite surrounding the lodge. This fresh spring water is served to diners and even used for baths, one more reason to savor this hidden Sierra treasure.

Rails, Tales and Trails

TO DONNER SUMMIT

Continue on Highway 40 east as it wends past fantastic granite formations and the Yuba River, and gives you a real feel for the lay if the land. Of course there are two seasons at this altitude, construction and winter, so don't be in a hurry and expect traffic delays.

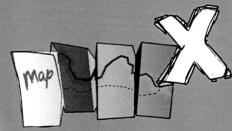

Rails, Tales and Trails

Twain on the Train

Rail Tales

During his "roughing it" stage of life in California and Nevada Mark Twain traveled through much of northern California by foot, horse, boat, stage coach and train. He took a trip on the Central Pacific Railroad while workers were drilling through the summit tunnel. That meant he had to get off the train at Cisco and find alternative transportation the rest of the way over the mountain to Truckee. The trip was in May, 1868 at the end of a long hard winter. The 32-year old Twain was shocked by the change in scenery and weather he experienced during his trip. Below is his description.

Up Among the Clouds, May 1868

the Summit of the Sierras—From Flowers to Snow Drifts

"I rather dread the trip over the Sierra Nevada tomorrow. Now that you can come nearly all the way from Sacramento to this city by rail, one would suppose that the journey is pleasant enough, but it is not. It is more irksome than it was before — more tiresome on account of your being obliged to shift from cars to stages and back again every now and then in the mountains. We used to rattle across all the way by stage, and never mind it at all, save that we had to ride thirty hours without stopping.

The other day we left the summer valleys of California in the morning — left grassy slopes and orchards of cherry, peach and apple in full bloom — left strawberries and cream and vegetable gardens, and a mild atmosphere that was heavy with the perfume of flowers; and at noon we stood seven thousand feet above the sea, with snow banks more than a hundred feet deep almost within rifle-shot of us. We were at Cisco, the summit of the Sierras, where for miles the railway trains rush along under tall wooden sheds, built to protect them from snows and the milder sort of avalanches. We had been running alongside of perpendicular snow-banks, whose upper edges were much above the cars. At Cisco the snow was twenty or thirty feet deep. I said to an old friend who lives there:

"Good deal of snow here."
"No — there ain't now — but we had considerable during the winter."
"Without meaning any offense, what might you call 'considerable'?"
"Sixty-eight feet on a dead level, and more a falling!"
"Good morning."
"Good morning — stay awhile?"
"Excuse me. My time is limited."

Rails, Tales and Trails

He spoke the truth. And yet he had the hardihood to spend two years there. Leaving Cisco, they sent us twenty four miles in four-horse sleighs, around and among the tremendous mountain peaks, grand with their regalia of storm-clouds. We swept by the company's stables on a level with their roofs, so deep was the snow.

Taking the advice of people I deemed wiser than myself, I had wrapped up myself in overcoats, and put on overshoes. But here in the midst of these snowy wastes the sun flamed out as hot as August, and I had to take off everything I could. It was a perfect tropical day. I got badly sunburned, and partly snow-blind, and I sweated more and growled more than I had in a year before. All this in a four-horse sleigh, in the midst of snow full twenty feet deep!

All I wish to say is, that I do not despise to go sleighriding in the summer time. And the next time I have to do such a thing I mean to have a fan, and some ice cream, and a suit of summer linen along.

The railroad is progressing rapidly. It is promised that those who take the Overland well along toward July, shall go hence to Chicago in eight days."

Twain was a noted weather observer, famously saying "the coldest winter I ever spent was a summer in San Francisco."

Soda Springs

Elevation 6,768 feet
Directions:
Off 80 at Exit 174

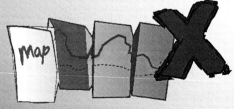

A stop at the Donner Summit Historical Society in Soda Springs will help orient you to the many historical and geographic wonders of this area. The Society is at the flashing yellow light on Donner Pass Road.

Rails, Tales and Trails

THE SUMMIT VALLEY is today home to a thriving seasonal recreational community with several alpine lakes and ski resorts. Take a side tour to Serene Lakes, off Soda Springs Road (look for the flashing yellow light — it's the only one around). The conjoined alpine lakes, Serena and Dulzura, were supposedly given their delightful names by Mark Twain, but then again almost every small town says Twain worked at its newspaper, so be careful of such harmless claims. The lakes are beautiful, uncrowded, and you can take a nice easy lunchtime hike around them. Soda Springs was once called Hopkins Springs, founded by Mark Hopkins who envisioned it as a tourist destination. There still is, I hear, a cabin that Hopkins built, and an exclusive enclave down a steep canyon secreted behind "no trespassing" signs. I have not been there, but apparently very famous people have. That's your clue and all I'm going to say. I'm adventurous but I'm not saying anything else. Explore on your own.

Also here is the famed **ROYAL GORGE CROSS COUNTRY SKI RESORT,** the largest cross country ski resort in America with over 200 km of groomed trails. It offers open, majestic views of the Sierra terrain. **To get there turn onto Soda Springs Road, turn right onto Pahatsi and into the Royal Gorge parking area.**

Rails, Tales and Trails

THE TUNNELS AT DONNER SUMMIT

Elevation 7,100 feet

Directions:

From Rainbow Lodge take Highway 40 east, or go back to I-80 and exit at Soda Springs, it's about 5 miles to the summit. Drive to the Rainbow Bridge Donner Lake overlook and park there or park on the side of Highway 40.

Rainbow Bridge was completed in 1926 and has been offering tourists from around the world spectacular views since then. The information signs here have a quick recap of the area's history and will help you orient yourself to the Summit environment. Look to the right and you will see the old rail route snaking through the tunnels around the lake on the ridge clinging to the side of the mountain. It is necessary to bring good hiking boots, water and a powerful flashlight to get the most out of this experience. Head back west, in the opposite direction from Donner Lake, and you will find a series of markers commemorating the tunnels.

The most impressive and spectacular aspect of the Central Pacific Railroad route are the Donner Summit tunnels, and you can get an appreciation for the vision, effort and achievement involved in completing the seminal engineering and construction project of the 19th Century. The tunnels are not currently used and there are not any rails through the tunnels.

Rails, Tales and Trails

In the 1920s the railroad blasted a new tunnel through nearby Mount Judah and over time stopped operating in these old tunnels. The longest tunnel is 1,659 feet and the shortest 92 feet and they all posed an incredible challenge to the railroad engineers and construction crews. The crews had to blast through granite, much harder to deal with than marble or lime-stone, and harder than steel. Granite is durable, seemingly impervious to wind and water and you will be amazed, as I was, to put your hands in the 150-year old drill holes that appear to have been made yesterday.

As challenging as the mountain terrain and the granite proved to be, it was a much softer element — snow – that almost proved to be the project's undoing. The railroad's visionary engineer, Theodore Judah, knew exactly how rough the Sierra winter could be. Judah made a close examination of the snow, and thought it could be brushed aside by powerful train engines. But no mechanical device was powerful enough to handle the sometimes 60 or 70 feet of wet, thick "Sierra Cement" (so called because of the high water content in the flakes) that can descend on the Summit. Howling winds create snow drifts dozens of feet high, increasing the chances for avalanches. In 1866-1867, a howling winter smothered the summit. The timber trestle at Cisco buckled and collapsed. Workers carved snow tunnels to get from camp to the granite tunnels to keep working. It became clear to the railroad owners that a solution had to be found to conquer the snow or the

entire operation was in jeopardy. The solution was to build strong wooden show sheds that would link the tunnels – a total of 37 miles in a 40-mile mountainous stretch. It would take 65 million feet of timber and 900 tons of iron bolts and spikes at a cost of $2 million, a staggering cost but one that railroad executives said "will pay for their cost in a single winter."

The wooden sheds proved to be an expedient solution and worked to keep the lines open during the winters. But they were prone to being set on fire by embers from the wood-burning steam engines. And as anyone who lives in the mountains knows, harsh winters are hell on structures. An army of track walkers and snow shovlers kept the tunnel passages open and the tracks clear of ice. Fire lookouts kept a sharp eye for blazes from above and sent fire train

Rails, Tales and Trails

crews hurtling down the tracks to extinguish the fires before they could devour miles of sheds. Carpenters made continuous repairs. It is said that many workers lived in old freight cars, seldom seeing the light of day from their snow-encased universe.

Today the sheds are gone, only old randomly-scattered timbers can be found. The railroad keeps the way open with enormous "flangers" and "spreaders" that move tons of snow from the tracks. On rare occasions, the massive rotary snowplow, a behemoth invented in the 1880s, is unleashed to cut through the snow. Even with all the modern technology and massive horsepower, Mother Nature can still conspire to close the tracks today.

The Central Pacific built tunnels 3 through 13 in the Sierra in 1867. Seven of the tunnels are in a two-mile stretch east of Donner Summit, and you will notice they are mostly located on places where the track curves.

You are in an area of hikers, rock climbers, ski resorts and spectacular views. Pink, red, blue and white wildflowers carpet the sides of hiking trails. The Central Pacific construction is just one of many interesting things to see at Donner Summit. You can find ancient Native American petro glyphs on the large granite slabs and an exhibit that explains the origins of the ancient art. You can also see where wagon wheels left ruts on the rocks, relics of the *Dutch Flat-Donner Lake wagon road* that was built in 1863. One more thing to look for is the elusive Chinese catfish. It is said that Chinese workers stocked ponds near the rail construction sites with catfish to provide fresh fish for their meals. I have never seen catfish in the ponds, but if you happen upon a few you will know they have been swimming here for 150 years or so.

Rail Tales: On the north side of Highway 40 you will see "rock people" lounging, the work of a local artist. A great resource to check out is the website "On The Summit" http://onthesummit.net/wordpress/activities/trails/donner-pass-history/. It tells of a variety of hiking trails and activities on the Summit, and is run by George Lamson and Linda Cashion, supported by their two golden retrievers, Calla and Maggie.

ROCK SCRAMBLING TO THE TUNNELS

Don't be dissuaded by the sight of rock climbers making vertical ascents of the rock face. You can see where the smooth rock meets the roadway. You can walk up the rocks to the ridge above you. It's not the Great Wall of China here but you will find the Chinese wall, actually two walls built to hold the trains that crossed the mountains for more than a century. A plaque commemorates the work of the Chinese who blasted and scraped the tunnels through the mountain and built this wall that held the heavy train loads through the 1990s. It reads:

Rails, Tales and Trails

China Wall of the Sierra marker
"Charles Crocker, Construction Chief of the Central Pacific Railroad (CPRR), contracted for a workforce of approximately 12,000 Chinese laborers to push the CPRR tracks over its Trans-Sierra Crossing on its race east to a meet with the Union Pacific at Promontory, Utah Territory. A railroad retaining wall and fill, constructed of Sierra granite, stand silently above on the pass as a lasting monument to the Asian "Master Builders" who left an indelible mark on the history of California and the West."

Initially the Big Four resisted hiring Chinese, but soon discovered the Chinese proved to be quick learners and excellent workers. Samuel Montague, the chief construction engineer reported that "some distrust was at first felt regarding capacity of this class for the services required but the experiment has proved eminently successful. They are faithful and industrious. Many of them are becoming very expert in drilling, blasting and other departments of rock work." Stanford, in a report to President Andrew Johnson said "as a class they are quiet, peaceable, patient, industrious and economical. " There was no doubt Chinese workers had the right stuff and literally "made the grade" for the Central Pacific Railroad. The Chinese, using only picks and shovels, would sculpt the grade. Excavated dirt and rock were loaded into small carts and moved to the side or used as fill to construct a trestle. White workers would lay in the heavy rail, which were 25-feet long and weighed 560 pounds per rail. Workers made around $35 a month, paid in gold coin, not the less-desired paper greenbacks. The wages were good money compared to a Union private's pay of $13 a month.

Rails, Tales and Trails

There are about two miles of abandoned rail bed and tunnels located above the parking lot of Donner Ski Ranch resort adjacent to scenic and slow highway 40. This is the most scenic stretch of roadbed, yet for most tourists traveling on the railroad was a huge letdown. The tunnels and snow sheds made it seem like the tourists were railroading in a barn. The original Tunnel 6 (the Summit Tunnel) is a 1,659 foot long deep, dark cave. Inside you can see the solid granite that the workers attacked beginning in 1865. Snow can choke the entrances much of the year into late spring. Inside the tunnel the snow melt soaks the trail, and torrents of cold water come flowing through the rock. Many chisel marks and holes remain where the Chinese workers bored into the granite. They then inserted black powder and nitroglycerin and the powerful explosions blasted the granite loose. In some areas you can see where large chunks of the rock were blown to the side. The dark tunnels are eerie cathedrals, an evocative spot that offers reminders of the enormous human activity required to bore through the mountain. One can touch the holes bored to hold explosives and see the chisel marks where the stone was hewed with pick and shovel. I get a peaceful feeling deep inside the moist, cool tunnels, feeling a connection to that early age of heroics and hard work. Surely, these tunnels were hewn by men of a great generation.

Tunnel 6 was a staggering feat of engineering. It sits more than 7,000 feet above sea level. The surveyors were so accurate that the workers found they were only two inches off from perfect alignment when they broke through the final granite wall. On October 7, 1867, after Tunnel 6 was finished and before the first locomotive went through, federal rail inspectors proudly wrote this glowing report:

"The crest of the Sierra is pierced by a tunnel 1659 feet in length, 16 by 20 feet, through the hardest kind of blue granite, and the line opens on the slope facing the east upon the precipitous side of a high granite peak,.......and is a wonderful achievement in Railroad Engineering.....The laborers on the tunnel have been principally Chinese. They worked in gangs of three shifts of eight hours each per day laboring steadily day and night during the storms of one of the severest winters ever known in California, upon the summit of the highest mountain range in the United States and at an elevation greater by several hundred feet than the top of Mount Washington. The drilling is done entirely by hand laborer."

The work was very hard, and the debris and smoke from the blasting must have made the working conditions hot and dusty. There have been many legends, some incorporated into books, claiming that thousands of Chinese were killed in the construction. Railroad historian Chris Graves has closely examined source documents and believes that about 130 people died building the Central Pacific Railroad from the years 1863-1869. This does not include deaths from avalanches or men killed by disease or gunfights. The tunnel was "holed through" August, 30, 1867 and the first locomotive chugged through the tunnels in November 1867.

Rails, Tales and Trails

At the Sugarbowl Ski Academy immediately west of the summit in the parking lot (this is part of the Pacific Crest Trail) is a rock plaque commemorating the construction of the railroad, unfortunately hidden in the bushes, neglected. On top of the tunnel is a big slab of rusted metal. It is covering what was once a shaft from the top of the mountain. To work faster, the engineers decided to work all four tunnel faces at the same time. Two teams worked inward from the eastern and western ends of the tunnel and two more teams, sitting back-to-back, worked from the middle, moving outward. In order to lift the debris out of the middle of the tunnel, a train engine was dragged to the summit, bolted down and christened the "Black Goose." It was housed in a house or shack, and many timbers around the tunnel are thought to be from that original shelter.

Hiking in this area offers spectacular views of some of America's best scenery. Here is the famed crest of the Sierra, and glimmering in the distance beautiful Donner Lake. This is the granite crest, the road once thought impossible for the Central Pacific Railroad to reach, 100 rocky miles from Sacramento.

Rails, Tales and Trails

The Summit to Donner Lake

Here our trek begins to descend. From this point you will notice the rivers and streams heading east toward the Great Basin. But while the route is mainly downhill it still presented enormous engineering challenges, and more spectacular scenery. Standing in the parking lot at Rainbow Bridge you will get a gorgeous view of Donner Lake. To your right you will see the old train tunnels clinging to the ridgeline and paralleling Donner Lake. The old railroad grade from the summit to Donner Lake drops about 800 feet in a mile and is very dusty. You can hike to East Portal Tunnel but at that point the modern Union Pacific line takes over and you MUST NOT enter the tunnel. You will experience the same thrill a reporter felt when he took the first passenger train from Sacramento to Reno, and made this descent past Donner Lake. "The road winds around the precipitous mountainside, almost encircling Donner Lake as it descends, and following around a long canyon, making a circuit of seven miles to gain no more than a quarter of a mile, we reach the outlet of the lake. Now we descend rapidly on one of the most beautiful, smooth and solid roads on the continent into the romantic valley of the Truckee."

Rails, Tales and Trails

DONNER LAKE

Elevation 5,935 feet

Directions:
Continue on east Donner Pass Road
Drive carefully. Fortunately there are many turnouts
and you pull over and take in the view.
At the bottom of the twisting road is Donner Lake, a
popular tourist destination.

This is a spectacular road offering alternating mountain and lake vistas. The road winds over the canyon precipitously, and is often closed in bad weather. Drive carefully. Fortunately there are many turnouts and you pull over and take in the view. At the bottom of the twisting road is Donner Lake, a popular tourist destination. The three-mile long lake offers a full range of winter and summer recreational activities, and a nice sandy beach. Restaurants and pubs are abundant, and the average 75 degree summer temperature makes Donner Lake a summer paradise. Of course, the region was not always so hospitable to travelers, as we will find out shortly.

PIONEER MONUMENT AT DONNER STATE PARK

Directions:
Continue past the lake to the entrance to the park.
Or take I-80 exit 184 for Donner Pass Road.

The California State Parks Department calls the Donner Party "the dark side of the American Dream." (Cruel reminders pop up even today; as I was writing "Donner Party" my spell check kept suggesting "Dinner" party.) If any event in California history has more myth and legend around it than the transcontinental railroad it's the Donner Party. An early snowstorm in 1846 trapped the travelers. "Forty-one of the 89 would-be settlers perished. When their provisions and oxen were consumed, the desperate emigrants cannibalized their dead friends and relatives." According to the state park's website the park "is located where many members of the Donner Party spent their final days. Rangers report that about two hundred thousand visitors, most very curious about the cannibalism aspect of the Donner story, stop at the state park each year."

Rail Tales: Many people think the statue in the park depicts the Donner tragedy. Actually, it's the "Pioneers of the West" monument sculpted by John MacQuarrie, the sculptor of the Theodore Judah monument we met in Old Sacramento. The monument depicts a man and a woman optimistically looking west, into the sun. The woman holds a baby while a young child peeks from behind her father's leg. They are peering into a bright California future.

This great monument was funded by private subscriptions. Backers of the project took splinters from the Donner Party cabin, placed them in small glass containers and sold them for one dollar apiece to pay for the monument. Upon his death the obituary in the San Francisco Chronicle called MacQuarrie a "widely known sculptor and muralist" who had won "particular fame for his Donner Lake monument."

The Emigrant Trail Museum, located at Donner Memorial State Park, takes about an hour to visit. The park has about 2.5 miles of hiking trails. Park property in Coldstream Canyon to the south lines up with the primary Emigrant Trail, which leads up to U.S. Forest Service and the Pacific Crest trails beyond the park. Hiking up these trails offers views of the current and old railroad grade. You can find detailed maps in the museum.

TRUCKEE

Elevation 5,817 feet

Directions:
The Lincoln Highway/Donner Pass Road will take you right into Truckee, one of the most important Central Pacific Railroad towns.

Historic Truckee lies nestled in the mountains in a climate that is almost subarctic and averages more than 204 inches of snow a year, making it one of America's snowiest cities. In order to lay the rail line into Nevada as quickly as possible, the Central Pacific leapfrogged the summit tunnels which were still being bored through, and built a separate link following the Truckee River. That made Truckee a major supply hub. An army of workers arrived and 25 lumber mills sprung up to support the Central Pacific Railroad construction into Nevada. In early 1867 crews hauled material over the summit on wagons, a total of 20 tons of iron, engines and flat cars pulled around the construction area to Truckee.

Truckee today is a busy spot of some 16,000 souls, many drawn for skiing, hiking and the recreational lifestyle. High ridgelines surround the town, offering great views and photo opportunities. Walking around, you will see a great mix of architecture from small homes clustered next to the railroad tracks to larger Victorians. Quaint shops feature hand-crafted goods, and I love the feel at **Moody's Bistro and Lounge in the Truckee**

Hotel at 10007 Bridge St, just a block or so from the Amtrak station, which has played host to visitors for well over a century. The small stage and intimate setting are a welcome respite after a long day outdoors, and live music adds to the ambiance. Built in 1873, the hotel has attracted its share of celebrities over the years, but one of its best nights ever was in March, 2004 when Paul McCartney and his wife stopped by for dinner during a ski vacation. Sir Paul couldn't resist jumping on stage and pounding out a few jazz numbers with Tahoe musician George Souza. Another favorite spot also loaded with history is the **Cottonwood Bar and Restaurant** that overlooks downtown Truckee from one of the nation's oldest ski lodges at **10142 Rue Hilltop Road.** I always linger over the historical artifacts, local photographs and artists' works that line the walls. You can dine on the large wooden back porch that offers stunning views of Truckee and the mountains that ring it - sunsets here are unforgettable, and the food is great. Even the cool mountain air is made manageable by the quilts hung on the wall available for the diners to wear on cool nights. The land on which the Cottonwood stands was originally owned by Charles Crocker.

Jax at the Tracks is a more affordable, but no less fun eatery down the hill from the Cottonwood hugging the railroad tracks at **10144 West River Street.** A classic diner, it was hauled from Philadelphia to Truckee, then restored. Jax proudly boasts decadent comfort food, and I can attest you will feel sufficiently fortified after plowing through its legendary selection of

burgers, steaks, fries and onion rings. Open for breakfast, lunch and dinner.

The **Truckee Railroad Museum is located next to the historic railroad station in downtown Truckee, at 10075 Donner Pass Road.** Located in a caboose, the museum features colorful displays on the importance of the railroad in the development of the region's natural resources. Trains frequently pass through the center of town offering some great opportunities to take pictures. "With its proximity to the Sierra Nevada summit, its vast forests, and its natural transfer point for passenger and freight traffic, south to Lake Tahoe and north to the Sierra Valley, Truckee would remain a railroad town of great importance for many decades," wrote Gordon Richards of the Truckee Donner Historical Society. "During the 1870's Truckee shipped more freight than any other point on the Central Pacific."

TRUCKEE RIVER CANYON FROM TRUCKEE TO NEVADA STATE LINE

I-80 up, down, around and east
(River diversion)

While the route you have taken from the west is steep and spectacular, it has been described by geologists as a "long and plannar [a geology term for being on a plane surface] western slope" with a "plunging escarpment [steep slope] facing east." You are now headed toward the escarpment. Hang on.

Rail Tales:
The Truckee River provides great white-water rafting and tubing. If you want a quick diversion from following the railroad, you can find one nearby. A favorite spot along the river is the **River Ranch Lodge and Restaurant in Tahoe City, just 15 miles south from Truckee on Highway 89 following the river's course.** You can rent a raft here and float gently down the river soaking in the sun or being ambushed by squirt-gun wielding pirates prowling the waters. You will float right into River Ranch and its wonderful summer outdoor barbeque.

The Truckee River flows out of Lake Tahoe at Tahoe City and runs north to Truckee. This is a pleasant stream favored by folks floating slowly on inner tubes and rubber ducks. At Truckee it then takes a right-hand turn east to Reno, and the river becomes a powerful force passable by only the most able of whitewater experts. This stretch of the trail was so rough the pioneers after first using it learned to avoid it. In 1844 the Stevens-Murphy-Townsend party, the first to take wagon trains over the Sierra Nevada, struggled through the canyon. In 1845 Caleb Greenwood and his sons found a new route that by-passed the Truckee River Canyon by leaving the river near Verdi, Nevada and following a ravine northwest over a 6,200 foot pass before circling into Truckee. This was about ten miles longer but preferable to dealing with the "torturous and boulder-strewn" canyon. This "Dog Valley" route remained the main emigrant trail until the Central Pacific Railroad came along. Finding the "Dog Valley" trail too steep, they headed down the river gorge.

The fast-flowing, narrow and shallow river carved a spectacular canyon that the railroad followed east from Truckee into Nevada. You will follow it on I- 80 to Verdi, Nevada. You are in for a twisting 22 mile road with spectacular views. The canyon walls seem to press against you as you make the magnificent descent on the backside of the Sierra Nevada. This is the "dry side" of the mountains, most of the snow having been dumped on the higher-elevation western slopes, and you will notice the soaring granite mountains starting to yield to large volcanic ash hills. Looking down from 80 you can see the modern rail line running next to the Truckee River at the bottom of the canyon. You will also notice a series of wooden flumes that carry water. In winter the water dripping from the flumes creates the image of giant beards dripping from the canyon's steep walls. The railroad laborers would need lots of wood to do the job, and loggers fed their harvest to sawmills that sprouted along the river to supply timber for bridges and ties. Two short tunnels and five bridges were built by the thousands of workers who battled snow and steep terrain.

Lumber and ice businesses were created by the Central Pacific, and up until the early 1900s the Truckee canyon was a thriving, vibrant commercial center with small towns and communities. Most of those towns are gone today, but there are a few stops worth making.

Rails, Tales and Trails

BOCA

Elevation 5,528 feet
Directions:
Take 80 east about 7.5 miles to the Hirshdale Road Exit.

This was the Central Pacific's Camp 17 and construction crews camped where the Little Truckee flowed into the Truckee, and the camp soon came to be called Boca, which is Spanish for mouth. The spot is best known today for the Boca Reservoir, which provides recreation year round. But it is one cold place, January 20, 1937, the temperature at Boca fell to -45°F (-43°C), the coldest temperature ever recorded in California.

These cold temperatures made it possible for the railroad to engage in one of its many side businesses. Before refrigeration ice was harvested from the mountain lakes, and sent to San Francisco and Sacramento, where California's famous fruits and vegetables could be packed in ice and sent across the country. It was reported that the company had ample facilities for storing enough ice in a single winter to supply California for a dozen years. In the parking area above the reservoir is a marker that says, "in the winter the log pond froze over. The company began harvesting the natural ice in 1869. The combination of the railroad and ice made Boca an ideal location for a brewery." In 1875 a brewery was established and became famous for its award-winning lager beer. The marker also has directions to a nearby Boca town site interpretive trail. I did not take the trail the January day I stopped by it was way too cold!

FLORISTON

Elevation 5,800 feet

Directions:
From Boca, take I-80 5.5 miles east down the canyon.
You will exit on a winding road that takes you to a narrow one-lane metal tunnel. Go through it and follow the steep road up the hillside, traveling through a second tunnel. Take the street to the top for spectacular canyon views. The Truckee River flows past the town at the bottom of the canyon.

Floriston was once home to one of the largest paper mills in the world, but now counts just 73 residents tucked away in homes on the steep hillside. It's a nice quiet spot that gives you a great view of the terrain the track layers dealt with in this area.

MISSING GOLD IN VERDI, NEVADA

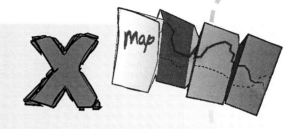

Elevation 4,905 feet

Directions:
Get back on 80 and head east into Nevada.
In ten miles you will come to Verdi,
site of the first train robbery on the Pacific Coast.

It's now a bedroom community for Reno, but has a wild west past. On November 5, 1870 at one in the morning five masked gunmen jumped aboard the train as it was leaving the Verdi station. The robbers, members of the Jack Davis gang, held the train crew at gunpoint. Breaking into the express car the robbers took $41,000 in gold from the Wells Fargo sacks. Wells Fargo, the Central Pacific Railroad, and the State of Nevada, posted a reward of $40,000.

The robbers fled in the early morning darkness and it wasn't until 8 am that a massive manhunt could be organized. It took a few days but the lawmen tracked the criminals down, but not before they were said to have buried some of the stolen gold along the north bank of the Truckee River, between Reno and Laughton's Hot Springs near the site of the long-abandoned River Inn. So far treasure hunters have not found any missing gold, and rumor has it many a brave soul has been scared off the treasure trail by Jack's nasty spirit.

RENO, NEVADA
Elevation 4,400 feet

Directions: Take 80 east 11 miles to Reno, called "The Biggest Little City in the World" due to the tall casinos that dominate the landscape.

The place that was to become Reno gained notoriety in the late 1840s and 1850s when thousands of travelers on their way to the California gold fields would rest in a lush spot fed by five year-round streams, the largest of which is the Truckee River. This marshy spot was known as Truckee Meadows, and the pioneers rested and fed their oxen and horses before launching the final push across the Sierra Nevada.

Reno was established on May 9, 1868 when the railroad obtained the property from a local entrepreneur and a 35 acre town site was laid out. But a series of fires over the years erased most of the original Central Pacific sites.

Rails, Tales and Trails

In the 1920s the Southern Pacific built a depot that today houses **the Amtrak depot, at 280 N. Center Street.** It is housed in a Mediterranean-style center building. Features include five tall, rounded arches that give form to graceful door and window openings. The building's two wings extend to the east and west and feature inset panels with decorative touches above the windows. Inside are chandeliers with Art Nouveau designs on the walls and large glass windows. The former passenger area features a terrazzo floor, wood-paneled ceiling and wooden benches. While digging a train trench, early Reno artifacts were unearthed, and are on permanent display in the Amtrak station at track level.

SPARKS, NEVADA

This pleasant Reno suburb grew from sagebrush surroundings to a modern suburb of almost 100,000 people. Sparks was created around 1900 when the Southern Pacific Railroad (SP) realigned its route and shifted operations from Reno to Sparks. Legend has it that the town was originally named after legendary capitalist E.H. Harriman who in the early 1900s was president of the Union Pacific and the Southern Pacific. On a trip west, Harriman allegedly rolled through the dusty frontier town that bore his name and politely but firmly declined the honor of having such a crude outpost named for him, so the people renamed it in honor of then-sitting Nevada Governor John Sparks.

In 1903-1904, the railroad built the largest roundhouse in the world in Sparks. Check out the **Sparks Museum and Cultural Center at 814 Victorian Avenue.** A vintage steam locomotive, cupola caboose and Pullman executive car are displayed along with a depot replica.

Rails, Tales and Trails

END OF AN ERA

East of Reno the railroad would not have to build any tunnels and just five bridges all the way across Nevada. It had taken five years to complete the 154 miles of track from Sacramento to Reno. It took just ten months to build the remaining 536 miles to Promontory, Utah. The Union Pacific met the Central Pacific May 10, 1869, a date that is one of the most famous in American history. How well did the California-based railroad do its job? Among the first to ride from Omaha to Sacramento was Army Captain John Charles Currier. He described the Union Pacific portion of the trip as very shaky and even fell down once due to the coarse ride. Captain Currier attended the ceremony at Promontory and transferred to the Central Pacific line for the rest of the trip. In his diary he noted the fast and smooth ride the Central Pacific Railroad offered into California. "At Humboldt Wells, Nevada Territory, 165 miles from Promontory. We are making excellent time. There is a perceptible difference in the running time from that of the U.P. We go faster....We run thirty miles per hour with very few stops. The Centrals carry their water along with them in immense tanks for it is very difficult to get water here. The grading of the road is perfect: for the last 80 miles we have run as smooth as a floor.

With all this we ran like lightening at a frightful speed. Made 200 miles last night. Sometimes our car, it being the rear one would snap as if it was a whip. Several of [his fellow army] officers became alarmed at our speed. On, On we rushed without a stop....All remark on how well this road is built, certainly fifty percent better than the U.P....The "C.P's" don't mean to keep us long on their road. They halt for nothing and seem impatient if we wish to stop for coffee. Somewhat different from the 'U.P.' " We don't often think of the world before mechanization as one we would want to inhabit. But envision the people who lived in the west before the railroad came. They ran stagecoaches and freight businesses; the word teamster comes from the people who ran teams of oxen and horses and moved the freight by wagon. In the timber industry the teams would pull felled trees out of the deep dark canyons to the mills that dotted the landscape. But once the railroad came the small mills were closed. Worlds collapsed, jobs disappeared. A Tahoe-area bullwhacker named Dan McNeil understood his world was changing forever. I imagine him as a big, strong man, smart enough to handle the "slobs" that worked for him and tough enough to manage the huge oxen (the bulls) that labored under his direction. He left this poem that revealed an era now long past:

"Then I was king of the whole woods-crew,
And I ruled with an iron grip;
And never a slob on the whole dam' job
Dared give me any lip.

But now, alas, my days are past;
There's no job for me here.
My bulls are killed and my place is filled
By a donkey engineer.

Instead of my stately team of bulls
All stepping along so fine,
A greasy old engine toots and coughs
 And hauls in turn with the line."

Life also changed for the workers who labored on the road. When the Central Pacific construction reached Reno, about half of the Chinese workers, about 6,000, were laid off. With the heavy work over the mountains completed, there was no need for so many men. But the Central Pacific made sure their contribution was recorded in history. A San Francisco newspaper reported that "J.H. Strobridge, when the work was all over, invited the Chinese ... to dine at his boarding car. When they entered, all the guests and officers present cheered them as the chosen representatives of the race which have greatly helped to build the road," said Charles Crocker, chief of construction."I wish to call to your minds that the early completion of this railroad we have built has been in large measure due to that poor, despised class of laborers called the Chinese, to the fidelity and industry they have shown."
They went to other jobs in California, some continuing to work for the railroad as it expanded south and east, while others found work in different construction projects, including digging wine caves in the hills of Napa (next time you are wine tasting look for them at Schramsberg and Beringer Vineyards.)

But the road was done and commerce and trade flourished. Agriculture blossomed as farmers were able to ship fruits and vegetables to the big cities of the east. Hotels and restaurants sprung up to accommodate the tourists who traveled to California to see the wonders they had heard about. A trip that had taken four months and cost about a thousand dollars now cost just $150 and could be completed in a week. According to Freight Capital, "the completion of the transcontinental railway resulted in over $50 million worth of freight shipped from one side of the nation to the next on a yearly basis, or nearly $1 billion dollars in 2002 dollars. Besides being able to ship across country, the railroad also opened up opportunities for foreign goods to ship across the nation from either side. This meant Asian goods could easily travel to the east and European goods found their way west. With the building of the first continental railway, new areas and regions of the country were open to production and industry, and the American dream began in earnest. America experienced a production boom with its first 'technological' corridor'."
MacQuarrie, Jane and Leland Stanford, Dr. Strong, "Smiler" Colfax, Hopkins, the Chinese workers, Strobridge, E.B. and Margaret Crocker and all the others are largely forgotten now, but their generation must surely be in the running for America's Greatest. In this book I hope I have helped preserve their memories and the stories behind their great accomplishments. There may be no better summary of their era than the words on the Pioneer monument that stands tall and strong near Donner Summit:

 "VIRILE TO RISK AND FIND;
KINDLY WITHAL AND A READY HELP.
FACING THE BRUNT OF FATE; INDOMITABLE,—UNAFRAID."